RAISING A SOCIALLY SUCCESSFUL CHILD

ALSO BY STEPHEN NOWICKI

Choice or Chance: Understanding Your Locus of Control and Why It Matters

Will I Ever Fit In?

Teaching Your Child the Lanuguage of Social Success

Starting Kids Off Right: How to Raise Confident Children Who Can Make Friends and Build Healthy Relationships

Helping the Child Who Doesn't Fit In

RAISING A SOCIALLY SUCCESSFUL CHILD

TEACHING KIDS *the* NONVERBAL LANGUAGE THEY NEED *to* COMMUNICATE, CONNECT, *and* THRIVE

STEPHEN NOWICKI

Little, Brown Spark
New York   Boston   London

TO MY WIFE, KAAREN
WHOSE LIFE IS A TESTIMONY TO THE MEANING
OF STRENGTH, GOODNESS, AND COURAGE

Copyright © 2024 by Stephen Nowicki

Hachette Book Group supports the right to free expression and the value of copyright. The purpose of copyright is to encourage writers and artists to produce the creative works that enrich our culture.

The scanning, uploading, and distribution of this book without permission is a theft of the author's intellectual property. If you would like permission to use material from the book (other than for review purposes), please contact permissions@hbgusa.com. Thank you for your support of the author's rights.

Little, Brown Spark
Hachette Book Group
1290 Avenue of the Americas, New York, NY 10104
littlebrownspark.com

First Edition: March 2024

Little, Brown Spark is an imprint of Little, Brown and Company, a division of Hachette Book Group, Inc. The Little, Brown Spark name and logo are trademarks of Hachette Book Group, Inc.

The publisher is not responsible for websites (or their content) that are not owned by the publisher.

The Hachette Speakers Bureau provides a wide range of authors for speaking events. To find out more, go to hachettespeakersbureau.com or email HachetteSpeakers@hbgusa.com.

Little, Brown and Company books may be purchased in bulk for business, educational, or promotional use. For information, please contact your local bookseller or the Hachette Book Group Special Markets Department at special.markets@hbgusa.com.

ISBN 9780316516471
Library of Congress Control Number: 2023946357

Printing 1, 2024

LSC-C

Printed in the United States of America

CONTENTS

Introduction: A New Kind of Trouble   1

Part 1: Nonverbal Communication • 23

Chapter 1: The Language of Relationships   25

Chapter 2: The Six Types of Nonverbal Communication   47
A Primer

Part 2: The Silent Orchestra • 63

Chapter 3: Rhythm   67
The Stealth Nonverbal Channel

Chapter 4: Facial Expressions   93
Smile and the World Smiles with You

Chapter 5: Personal Space   121
That's Close Enough

Chapter 6: Physical Touch   145
Proceed with Caution

Chapter 7: Vocalics   171
Can You Hear What My Words Aren't Saying?

Chapter 8: Body Language   195
The Traffic Cop at the Intersection

Conclusion   227

Acknowledgments   238
Notes   244
Index   257

INTRODUCTION

A New Kind of Trouble

Anyone who does anything to help a child is a hero to me.

— Fred Rogers

During the 1990s I found myself deeply involved in trying to solve a mystery. Troubled children who were being referred to my clinical psychology practice were struggling socially, yet their problems had no clear cause. One of my patients, a nine-year-old boy named Greg, was a good example. Greg seemed typical in almost every way imaginable. He got decent grades at school, could swing a bat as well as most kids his age, liked to run and play all kinds of games, enjoyed adventure-themed movies, and had a dog named Randy whom he'd taught to roll over and beg. His favorite meal was pizza with extra cheese and a giant Dr Pepper. Greg was neurotypical; he had no obvious learning, psychiatric, or

INTRODUCTION

developmental disorders. His dad, an accountant, and mom, who worked part-time at a clothing consignment shop, loved Greg, and though they wanted him to achieve in school, they didn't put excessive pressure on him. He attended a public school with a good reputation and had helpful, compassionate teachers.

And yet something was very wrong. Greg wasn't happy. He had no friends, and he couldn't understand why. None of the other kids seemed to want to run around and play with him or go with him to the movies or invite him over to eat cheese pizza with extra cheese. He didn't want to be alone, yet he was. Both his parents and his teachers were concerned enough about Greg to suggest an evaluation. That's where my colleague Marshall Duke and I became part of his story, and he became part of ours.

We began our clinical assessment by observing Greg at school, where he was experiencing the most social difficulties. On the playground at recess time, we immediately noticed that he walked around the periphery of the groups of children playing their games, never joining in. Others easily entered or left the games, but Greg stayed on the sidelines, looking lost. It was obvious that he wanted to play with the others, but all he could manage was hesitant observation. Later that afternoon, we asked Greg about his classmates. "The thing is," he said, "I like being with them. I just wish they liked being with me."

As fathers with children about Greg's age at the time, his answer broke our hearts. As clinical psychologists, we were perplexed. And Greg wasn't the only patient experiencing these issues; in fact, he was one of many. Another child, Lucy, was being picked on by her classmates for reasons that eluded both her teachers and her parents. Her parents had moved her to a new school because they suspected that her previous school, with unruly classmates and unhelpful teachers, had caused the problem. But she and her parents were now confronting the fact that a new environment, with a new group of children and new set of teachers, hadn't made any difference. The answer lay elsewhere.

Greg and his socially disconnected peers had no obvious intellectual, physical, or emotional shortcomings. What were they lacking? What were they doing wrong? My colleague and I were practicing clinical psychologists, but we were also extensively trained in scientific theory and research methodology. As it turned out, we would need both to solve the puzzle of why these children weren't fitting in.

LOOKING FOR CLUES

Like detectives at the center of any good mystery, we searched widely and diligently for clues. The first came through our experience as consultants to public school programs for neurodivergent children and adolescents. We knew that kids with developmental disabilities often struggled socially, behaving in ways that other children found off-putting. For these kids, nine times out of ten, their social problems had to do with their lack of nonverbal communication skills. Nonverbal skills are all the ways that people communicate with one another without using words: through facial expressions, body language, physical touch, tone of voice, the rhythmic back-and-forth of our interactions, and the amount of space we leave between ourselves and others. Children with developmental disabilities often have trouble with eye contact or lack the ability to fall into the rhythm of a conversation, and they may use personal space and body language inappropriately. We began to wonder if neurotypical kids like Greg and Lucy might also be struggling with these kinds of nonverbal skills that can be so vital to making and sustaining friendships.

The next clue that nonverbal communication might be associated with Greg's and Lucy's relationship struggles came from my interactions with young psychotherapy clients. I noticed that many of them would enter a therapy session with clenched fists and angry faces, but when I asked why they were angry or upset, they would respond with surprise and deny feeling that way. Verbally they were telling me that they felt happy or relaxed, but their body language told quite another story. As a young psychotherapist, I had trained with disciples of Harry Stack Sullivan, the father of American psychiatry, who suggested that children and adolescents who unknowingly communicated "incongruently"—that is, they sent one emotional message verbally while simultaneously sending a different one nonverbally—often struggle to form intimate friendships. I began to wonder if incongruent communication might be a factor in the social difficulties I was seeing in my clients.[1]

INTRODUCTION

At the same time, it was obvious that these children were completely unaware of how their nonverbal language was at odds with their words, and the negative effect it might be having on others. All these pieces of information gleaned from observing a variety of children began to fit together to form a clearer picture of why kids like Greg and Lucy might be struggling.

PUTTING IT TOGETHER

Back in the nineties, when I first met Greg and Lucy, it was widely assumed that—for any child who didn't have an obvious developmental, psychiatric, or learning disorder—nonverbal communication was an innate skill, something they instinctively learned to do in the same way that they might learn to crawl or walk.

Moreover, while the topic of nonverbal communication might occasionally pop up in a newspaper or magazine article—about how to discern secret signs that someone liked you, or how to tell if someone was lying—it wasn't believed to play a significant role in social relationships. Marshall Duke and I, however, were coming to a much different conclusion.

We decided to conduct a study in which we administered tests to children measuring their ability to identify emotion in facial expressions and tones of voice. And, indeed, we found that the poorer the children performed on these assessments, the more trouble they had making friends and feeling good about themselves. In other words, the children we studied were much more likely to be able to make friends and succeed socially if they could correctly identify and interpret nonverbal cues in faces and voices.

We continued to study this connection between nonverbal ability and social success until, in 1992, we published our findings in a book we called *Helping the Child Who Doesn't Fit In*, which drew on our research and clinical observations to address the struggles of children like Greg and Lucy, and many others who just couldn't seem to get relationships right. These children badly wanted other kids to like them, but the harder they tried, the more others pushed them away. "They're like pieces of a puzzle that do not fit in," we wrote at the time. "They are the 'square pegs,' the 'fifth wheels,' the ones who are picked last for teams, the children who sit alone in the corner of the playground wondering why others don't like them. Sometimes they're called hurtful names such as 'nerd,' 'geek,' and 'weirdo.' At other times they're treated as if they don't exist."[2]

We were certain we'd discovered something hugely significant — that children who struggle socially often have difficulties with nonverbal communication as well — and the media thought so too. We were invited to explain our discoveries to Oprah Winfrey, who devoted an entire show to our findings, and we presented our idea to national audiences on *Good Morning America* and *The Today Show*. Daniel Goleman later referenced us heavily in his bestselling book, *Emotional Intelligence*.[3] We were recognized for our research and

INTRODUCTION

clinical contributions by the American Psychological Association, and schools in the United States, Europe (especially Britain), and elsewhere around the world began implementing our recommended therapies for struggling kids with positive results.

The goal of our book was to put parents, teachers, speech therapists, psychologists, and school administrators on alert to something they haven't given much thought but that might be very important in determining whether children would be socially successful. We had only begun to scratch the surface of what needed to be known about the role nonverbal language plays in the social lives of kids, but it was a start.

We knew the world would change in ways that impacted how kids connect and engage with one another, but we never imagined that it would change radically enough to require a comprehensive overhaul of our methods and recommendations, along with a new call to action for parents, teachers, and all those who care about children's ability to develop positive, healthy relationships in childhood and throughout their adult lives. Until now.

This book will bring you up to speed on the most exciting developments in the field of nonverbal communication and skill development over the past two decades and introduce you to all the latest findings about the "language of social success." And it will provide you—parents, teachers, and caregivers alike—with a new approach to helping children succeed socially, at a time when it is needed more than ever.

INTRODUCTION

KIDS IN CRISIS

There's no doubt in my mind that when children learn this nonverbal "language of relationships," they have a greater chance of thriving in life. But giving our children this wonderful advantage is more challenging than it has been at any other point in history. The world of human interaction has changed dramatically since I was a child. When I was growing up, I was free to roam around my neighborhood with my friends for hours on end. Every neighbor knew my name and where I lived and greeted me with smiles when they saw me. I came from a large extended family, with grandparents, uncles, aunts, cousins, constantly in and out of our family home, and so my days were filled with the faces, voices, postures, gestures, rhythm, and yes, the touch of being with others. These varied communication styles provided me with an amazing number of examples of how to let others know how I felt and what to look for to find out what was going on inside of them.

Sadly, parents today have a much harder time exposing kids to such a rich array of relationships. Many of us live far apart from extended family in much more atomized living environments than the one I grew up in. What's more, screens have come to dominate all our days—children and adults alike—leaving our children with a lot less time to learn about the intricate nonverbal back-and-forth of relationships.

As I sit down to write this book in 2023, we are still in the midst of a global pandemic that has disrupted our children's

INTRODUCTION

lives in ways that seemed unfathomable just a few years before. Parents, educators, and groups that support children's psychological well-being have declared a mental health crisis, and many are deeply worried about the social and emotional developmental ground this generation of children has lost to Zoom schooling, masking, and prolonged periods of lockdown. Yet even before COVID-19 shut down their schools and their social lives, the youngest members of the most troubled generation in history, Generation Z (Gen Z), were already stressed to the max.

Statistics on loneliness rates in children prior to 2000 are sparse, but we now know that the number of children who feel isolated and adrift has risen dramatically during the twenty-first century, due in part to increases in social media, cell phone, and internet use. While most of us have felt isolated and down at one time or another, the kind of chronic loneliness these kids were experiencing can have serious social consequences.[4] Repeated failures to meaningfully connect with others can produce anxiety and even depression, and obsessing about botched efforts to connect may lead to feelings of dismay, frustration, or even anger toward others they perceive as making relationships harder to create.

In 2021, the first ever national survey of loneliness revealed that a staggering number of people of all ages were experiencing loneliness, even prior to the pandemic. But the loneliest of all were children between the ages of ten and twelve, with more than one out of ten admitting to feeling lonely most of the time.[5] Not surprisingly, the upsurge in loneliness parallels increased rates of anxiety and depression.

According to the National Survey of Children's Health, anxiety-related problems were found in about 3 in 100 children (ages two to seventeen) in 2007. By 2016, that number had more than doubled to well over *7 in 100*. Though rates of depression haven't been rising as steeply as rates of anxiety, the number of children who reported struggles with depression jumped more than 50 percent, from 2 in 100 children in 2007 to over *3 in 100* in 2016.

If that weren't bad enough, the decade between 2007 and 2016 saw a spectacular upswing in children diagnosed as conduct disordered. Conduct disorder is a term applied to children who show an ongoing pattern of aggression toward others as well as serious violations of rules and social norms at home, in school, and with peers. These rule violations may involve anything from patterns of misbehavior to breaking the law resulting in arrest. Compared to others, children with conduct disorder not only are more likely to have difficulty getting along with peers but often report being lonely as well. The number of kids to receive this diagnosis skyrocketed from 3 in 100 in 2007 to *7 in 100* in 2016.[6]

Then came the pandemic, which escalated what was already a serious set of problems into a full-blown crisis — one that will likely affect young people for years to come. In a 2020 article in the *Lancet*, British psychologist Samantha Brooks and her colleagues described how past pandemics had left a trail of psychological damage in the form of post-traumatic stress symptoms, confusion, anger, frustration, boredom, separation anxiety, and feelings of uncertainty, and it turns out that the COVID-19 pandemic is following suit.[7] An article published by Joan Hope describing the impact of the pandemic on children with disabilities opens with a message by Suzanne B. Goldberg, President Joe Biden's acting assistant secretary of education at the time, illustrating just how much stress and strain the past two years had brought on our children. Published in July 2021, the report Hope quoted, titled "Education in a Pandemic: The Disparate Impacts of COVID-19 on America's Students," revealed that nearly three in ten parents surveyed in a Gallup poll said their child was "experiencing harm to [their] emotional or mental health," with 45 percent citing the separation from teachers and classmates as a "major challenge." And educators, parents, and administrators across the country continued to cite social and emotional well-being as major challenges facing their students, especially those learning from home. Meanwhile, suicidal ideation was also on the rise among children and young adults, as shutdowns and social isolation undermined many students' mental and emotional well-being. Even those with less severe responses still overwhelmingly reported an increase in negative feelings during the pandemic, as did many of their parents.[8]

During the pandemic, rates of anxiety and depression in children doubled again in the United States, this time in just two years, whereas it had previously taken an entire decade.[9]

INTRODUCTION

And the United States is not alone. In 2022, the World Health Organization reported that this rise in children's mental health difficulties is a worldwide phenomenon, identifying social isolation as a probable precipitating factor.[10] In a telling study originating in China, researchers examined a sample group of 2,330 schoolchildren who were on lockdown for a little over a month—a relatively brief period compared to what American children had to tolerate. By the end of that month, more than 20 percent of the children, one in five, reported anxiety and depressive symptoms.[11]

Throughout the pandemic, I heard one story after another about children having meltdowns while cooped up at home. Worse yet were the stories of children who became detached, withdrawn, and unmotivated, transforming into "zombies," as their parents put it. One mother told me she felt stuck between a rock and a hard place because while she was concerned that her daughter was spending "all day and a good portion of the night connected to TikTok," her attempt to curtail use of the phone caused her daughter to burst into tears and protest she was too lonely without the connection the device gave her to others.

Meanwhile, there is evidence that pandemic-induced stress has hit children with poor social skills harder than others.[12] Throughout the pandemic, teachers lamented their inability to provide all children not only with adequate academic instruction but with social instruction as well. They were frustrated by their inability to connect with students in a meaningful way; in 2022, one researcher found that students returning to school after COVID 19 lockdowns were struggling with social interactions such as turn-taking and making friends while also experiencing delays in speech and language learning.[13] In a national survey of educators administered by the EdWeek Research Center in January 2022, 39 percent of respondents said that "compared to prior to the pandemic in 2019, the social skills and emotional maturity levels" of their current students are "much less advanced." Forty-one percent said their students were "somewhat less advanced" in those areas, and 16 percent said they were "about the same" as their pre-pandemic peers.[14]

One exhausted third-grade teacher I spoke to said she had trouble sleeping at night because she knew she was not able to provide her students with the social and emotional tools they needed more than ever during this difficult period. Yet it was the children who were having difficulties *before* the pandemic, she told me, that really kept her up at night. "They are the real victims in this crazy way I've had to try and teach over the past two years. Some were having trouble finding their way before, but now I'm afraid they are completely lost."

I've experienced this stress and frustration in my own teaching as well. I'm dealing with college students, most of them the older members of Gen Z, but they, too, are suffering. My fear is that without intervention, younger children who have fallen behind in their social and emotional development will struggle with these skills even more once they reach the age of my students (and thereafter).

When I meet with teachers, they often provide me with examples of what one called "pandemic pandemonium." One shared what she experienced during an in-person class that took place soon after virtual teaching ended. As she had done often in the past, she split the class into groups and told them to assemble in different areas of the classroom to work together on a simple project she had carefully described beforehand. The first unnerving thing that happened was...nothing. The children were silent. Rather than noisily making their way to the assigned work areas as she expected, children froze in place and had to be coaxed to move over and join their group. Once the students managed to assemble, she was further dismayed to find they had no idea of how to work with one another. They argued, they jostled, and they complained. Noticeably absent were smiles and laughter. Living under the constant isolation and stress of the pandemic had robbed them of the ability to enjoy being and working with their classmates.

But while incidents like these have become more common and more frequent as a result of the pandemic, they were occurring in pre-pandemic times as well. What this tells us is that masking, Zoom school, and lockdowns only exacerbated an existing problem, namely, *children aren't learning the social skills they need to thrive.*

Even before COVID isolation, children had far less access to the kinds of situations and interactions necessary for learning nonverbal skills than did previous generations, with more time being spent on the internet than on the playground, and more conversations taking place over text messages and group chats rather than over a shared activity or get-together.[15] While much of the focus of research into screen use has been on adolescents, recent attention has been directed toward evaluating the negative effect on younger children too. In one study following four-year-old children on their journey through elementary school, researchers from Lars Wichstrøm's psychological laboratory found that by eight years of age, children who spent more time on screens were less likely to rate highly in emotional intelligence.[16]

The impact that this decline in actual face-to-face interactions has had on nonverbal language ability cannot be underestimated. Consider the results from a 2019 study by Yalda Uhls, a professor at UCLA's Center for Scholars and Storytellers, which followed two groups of twelve-year-old girls on a somewhat brief summer camp experience. One group was allowed to bring their smartphones with them to camp; the other was not. Before and after the camp experience, both groups of girls completed a test that measured their ability to identify emotion in the facial expressions of their peers. Uhl found that, after just five days, the girls who left their smartphones at home *significantly improved* their scores, while those who took their phones with them did not. All it took to enhance this important skill, in this instance, was substituting screen time with person-to-person time for just five days.[17]

While it's not realistic in our digital age to wean young people off technology entirely, we do need to carefully examine which types of on- and offline experiences facilitate their growth as social beings and which interfere with it. There is still much we don't know about the effect of screens on our children, but *one thing we do know is that children learn nonverbal skills through face-to-face interaction with others—and that they are less able to learn those skills via the interface of a screen.* The less interaction, the less opportunity for learning. And the less skilled children are nonverbally, the more difficult it will be for them to succeed socially in childhood and beyond.

A CRUCIAL CROSSROADS

Our children have a basic need to feel connected to one another and to the important adults in their lives. And while there is no one explanation for why so many of our kids are struggling to connect, it's clear that one of the most significant factors has been the erosion of their nonverbal language skills—skills necessary for developing and deepening relationships with others. To become socially successful, children must know how to take turns in a conversation and how to make the appropriate eye contact when listening and speaking to others. They need to know how loud to talk in a classroom versus on the playground, how close they can stand next to others without making them uncomfortable, and when it's okay to link arms with a friend or classmate (and when it's not). They need to be able to sync up with another child's vocal rhythms and identify the emotions they—and others—are conveying in their facial expressions and tones of voice. And they need to know how to stand up straight with shoulders back to project confidence, nod and smile with encouragement when a friend is speaking, project a friendly face, even when not interacting with anyone, and all the other nonverbal skills necessary for connecting with and deepening relationships with others.

Unfortunately, today we are seeing more and more bright, academically successful, neurotypical children whose nonverbal communication skills aren't developing as they should be. And without the benefit of such skills, putting a child in a room with other kids and expecting them to make friends becomes nearly as unrealistic as handing a book to a child who doesn't know how to read and expecting him to understand the meanings of the words.

The good news is that nonverbal language is teachable at any age. These skills aren't binary—as in, a child either has the skill or she doesn't. They exist on a continuum, which means that whatever a kid's current skill level might be, there is always room for improvement, especially given that children will need to continuously acquire more advanced skills as they become older and seek more mature relationships. Nor are these skills all-or-nothing; most children will acquire certain nonverbal skills more easily than others. For example, some kids may be adept at reading facial expressions but be less skilled at picking up emotion in tones of voice, and vice versa. And just because a child may not have learned as much as they should have at earlier ages, it does not mean that they will be doomed to a lifetime of social rejection and isolation; it simply means that they need help catching up. It doesn't mean that there is something "wrong" with your child either. Just as a child who is a bit behind in math or reading may need a little extra help to get back up to grade level, a child who is lagging behind her peers in nonverbal ability can easily catch up with the benefit of extra instruction and guidance.

These crucial nonverbal skills might not be ones you've ever considered directly teaching your child. Like most parents, you've probably been hyperfocused on your child's verbal skills, celebrating when your baby uttered his first word or spoke his first sentence. I remember my wife and I excitedly memorialized our son Andy's first word in a diary we still have. Yet no one writes down the date that an infant first turns his head to gaze in the direction of someone's voice, or points at something for the first time, or successfully waits his turn before playing with a toy with another child, despite the fact that each is an important milestone in children's social and emotional development. At school, children are drilled in spelling, grammar, and writing and receive immediate feedback on whether their answers are right or wrong, yet are left to learn the nuances of nonverbal communication on their own, without the focus given to the shiny supernova of spoken words. We simply don't teach nonverbal skills in the same systematic, formalized way that we teach verbal language, and so children can very easily fall behind.

With nonverbal communication mostly flying under the radar, the majority of parents and caregivers have no idea how powerful their influence on a child's acquisition of nonverbal language can be. As a parent, you're probably exceedingly careful about the words you use and the thoughts you express around your children, lest they repeat those things at school or on the playground. But you may not give any thought to the nonverbal language you use—or how your children might be absorbing and mimicking those forms of expression—such as speaking in a monotone, or sitting with a slumped posture, or failing to make encouraging nods and smiles when listening to someone speak.

Like many attentive and loving parents, you may have no idea that your child had fallen behind when it comes to nonverbal skills—or perhaps you had some awareness that your child was struggling but just weren't sure what you could do to help. The good news is that nonverbal skills are easy to teach and easy for kids to learn; in fact, the research shows that with some awareness and practice, they can be fully mastered.

Raising a Socially Successful Child addresses the two greatest challenges we face in ensuring that our kids are equipped with the social and emotional skills they need to thrive: an increasingly online culture that deprioritizes face-to-face interaction, and the myriad effects of a pandemic that has kept young people isolated or masked during some of the most pivotal years of their social development. Unfortunately, these two forces have fed off each other, accelerating children's nonverbal decline. Whether they know it or not, parents, caregivers, and teachers all over the world are at a crossroads. The time to act is now.

As a parent, there is a great deal you can do to help, but teachers and school personnel play an equally important role in providing the kinds of supportive, corrective experiences children need. Schools, after all, are where children spend most of their day, interacting with their peers under the watchful gaze of teachers who can create innumerable and abundant opportunities for social learning and give children the experience, practice, and help they need to learn how to communicate better nonverbally.

Rather than trust that children will inevitably and naturally pick up these skills, you can play a crucial and active role in their nonverbal education. Throughout this book, you'll find simple tips and activities you can use to help your child improve her nonverbal abilities. These include how to show your child how to be respectful of the personal space of other children, how to help her learn to read emotional cues in facial expressions, how to use touch appropriately, and how to fall into the rhythm of turn-taking in conversations. These easy-to-follow teaching tools are backed by scientific theory and research and yield significant results—and they are designed to be simple and painless for parents and teachers to practice with kids.

My goal in writing this book is to support parents, caregivers, and educators as they help today's children negotiate the increasingly complex—but ultimately rewarding—task of relating to others as they venture out into the world, first as children, then as adolescents and young adults. This book will guide you in helping your child recover the social skills she may have lost during more than two years of pandemic life—and develop the more advanced skills she needs to tackle the enduring challenges she may face in the years ahead. With this foundation, not only will your child have a better chance of social and emotional success in childhood and adolescence, but she also will be better equipped to forge meaningful and

INTRODUCTION

long-lasting relationships and achieve workplace success as an adult.

As was the case for Greg and Lucy, the young children with the mysterious cause for their lack of friendships, a little practice is often all that is needed to address problem areas and improve a child's life. I believe this book can provide you with the knowledge and tools you need to do just that. It is my singular mission to make that happen.

PART 1

NONVERBAL COMMUNICATION

A Teachable Skill (That Every Child Should Master)

CHAPTER 1

The Language of Relationships

SOME YEARS AGO, AFTER I HAD JUST FINISHED GIVING A TALK about the importance of nonverbal communication at a local preschool, a concerned parent approached me about her four-year-old son, Jack. With an anxious look on her face, she explained that Jack was having trouble making friends at school. According to his teachers, it wasn't that he was mean or rude to his classmates; he just seemed to have a knack for annoying them. On my next visit to the school, I had a chance to observe Jack in the company of his classmates at various times of the day. At the end of my visit, I had to concede that he certainly had a way of upsetting his fellow students. The problem wasn't anything he said; rather it was how he interacted with others nonverbally. Jack was a world-class "space invader." In his interactions with his peers, he stood too close to them and then moved closer as time passed. Soon he was bumping into everyone around him, irritating them even more. Jack seemed to have little idea of the interpersonal havoc he was creating.

I felt his mother ought to have a chance to see what I was seeing, so I asked her to come along with me on my next visit to the school so we could observe Jack together. Sure enough, just as before, Jack crowded in on his classmates, who would either move as far away as they could the second they saw him coming or simply treat him as if he weren't there. As we watched these encounters, I explained to Jack's mother that Jack seemed to be unaware of the unspoken boundaries delineating personal space. She confessed that he might not have learned about this unspoken rule because he was an only child and hadn't had many chances to interact with other children before he began preschool. I suggested a couple of simple ways she could help him to understand personal space and be more conscious about respecting it. One of these involved having him sit in a chair or stand with a circle of masking tape about four feet in diameter—the appropriate distance for social interaction—placed on the floor. I met with Jack's mother a week later and she seemed pleased, reporting that the masking tape circle had done the job of making invisible spatial boundaries more visible to Jack. In fact, she said, they had great fun practicing how close or far away to stand. She even invited the next-door neighbor's child to come and play their "how far to stand away and how close to get" game. By bringing Jack's mistake into his awareness, and directly teaching him how to correct it, the social problem was soon resolved. When I returned to the school two weeks later, Jack was smiling a lot more and having a much more pleasant time with his classmates.

We all know children like Jack, kids who just can't seem to get life "right" at times. They really want others to like them, but the harder they try, the worse they seem to do. In most cases, their social problems aren't the result of a learning disability, autism, or any obvious disorder, but rather something so basic it is easy to overlook—they just haven't had enough opportunities to learn the nonverbal language skills critical to being socially successful. We often assume that the most popular kids are always the smartest or funniest or most attractive kids in the class, but in reality, they are simply the kids who have learned how to make interacting with them comfortable and easy.

Every now and again, we psychologists see cases of children for whom genetic, biological, or emotionally traumatizing events, especially in early childhood, can produce extreme difficulties in interpreting others' nonverbal signals and/or expressing themselves nonverbally. This is seen most clearly for children on the autism spectrum and those diagnosed with nonverbal learning disorders. My colleague Marshall Duke and I coined a term for significant nonverbal deficits, *dyssemias* ("dys" = difficulty; "semia" = signs: a difficulty in processing nonverbal cues).[1] Yet with the right approaches and consistent practice, even children with dyssemias can learn the nonverbal skills they need to improve the quality of their social interactions, providing clear evidence that every child, no matter their current skill level, can get better at using and understanding nonverbal language in the same way that any child can become more proficient in any other skill, like math or reading.

While Jack's story had a happy ending, I wondered then, as I do now, what would have happened if we *hadn't* uncovered the nonverbal shortcoming that was causing him to struggle socially? How would the consistent rejection have affected him emotionally as the months and years passed? How many of our children, like Jack, find themselves socially disconnected from their peers because they haven't developed the nonverbal skills they need to interact successfully? And why, despite its tremendous importance, do we still allow nonverbal communication to fly under our collective social radar?

A MATTER OF LIFE AND DEATH

From the moment we are born until we draw our last breath, we are forming relationships with those around us. The importance of these relationships cannot be overstated. As adults, we know that we need strong relationships to feel fulfilled, supported, and on solid ground. Conversely, if we struggle to make relationships work, it doesn't matter how rich or smart or attractive we are; we're going to have a harder time in life.

Relationships, in fact, are literally a matter of life and death. Research has repeatedly shown that infants who get enough to eat and drink but are not sufficiently nurtured by others' touch, positive facial expressions, and warm voices can develop what is called "failure to thrive" syndrome, in which lack of external stimulation deprives the brain of the activation it needs for healthy social and emotional development—and these infants lose weight and even, in extreme cases, die.[2] On a more positive note, research also shows that people who have better relationships are more likely to live longer and healthier lives.[3] One study found that patients undergoing open-heart surgery who were happily married were three times more likely to survive the surgery than those who weren't.[4] Sir Michael Rutter, the renowned British psychiatrist who studied resilience, found that kids coming from very challenging backgrounds end up doing well in life as long as they have just one good adult relationship, whether with a family member, a teacher, or someone in the community.[5]

We could not live for very long without relationships, but as Harry Stack Sullivan, the father of American psychiatry, argued, the benefits of relationships go beyond mere survival. Sullivan warned that one of the most painful and frightening experiences we can have as human beings is to feel alone, abandoned, or disconnected from others.[6] Or as the author and journalist Melissa Faye Greene has put it, "The difference between no friends and one good friend is like the difference between a pitch-black room and one lit by birthday candles."[7]

Sullivan was among the first major psychological practitioners and theorists to emphasize the important role relationships play in our emotional development, arguing that the most significant determiner of our behavior and personality is how we interact with others. Prior to his writings, the prevailing view was championed by Sigmund Freud, who was more concerned with what was going on inside of our "psychic" space.[8] Rather than emphasizing Freud's psychosexual stages, of oral, anal, phallic, latent, and genital, Sullivan believed our personality developed as a product of the increasingly complex social interactions we navigate over the course of our lives. According to Sullivan, childhood development is best understood as the process of learning the different relationship skills needed to progress from one milestone to the next as we move from less complex to more complex relationships. Each phase requires a unique set of skills, but the one thing that was consistent throughout all phases of development, he found, was the importance of nonverbal communication.[9]

It's a testament to the power of nonverbal communication that the bond between parent and child—probably one of the most intense and intimate relationships you will ever experience— is forged during the first year of life, before your child is able to utter or understand the meaning of a single word. In fact, infants are born with a rudimentary set of behaviors that seem designed to forge such bonds, by enticing others to pay attention to them in a nurturing way.[10] One could even call it a survival instinct, given that babies are entirely dependent on their adult caregivers for food, shelter, protection, and all the basic resources they need to survive. Whereas many other species adopt a "strength in numbers" strategy for survival of their young and produce thousands of eggs in hope that some few will survive by sheer chance, humans, along with most mammals, use a very different approach to guarantee their offspring will survive. They have fewer young, but they invest more energy, time, and attention to be sure that each one lives and thrives.

A few years back, this concept was brought home to me when I was lucky enough to spend some time in the lab of Philippe Rochat, a well-known developmental psychologist and colleague of mine at Emory University. Rochat was re-creating the famous "still face" experiment first carried out by the American psychologist Edward Tronick in 1975.[11] When Tronick began his studies, there was disagreement within the field about whether infants could manage the turn-taking and back-and-forth communication of an ongoing social interaction. Tronick's studies supported the idea that they can.

In his landmark study, Tronick had mothers playfully interact with their infants (who ranged in age from eight months to a year) for a couple of minutes before asking them to stop what they were doing and to be silent and still. No more smiles and happy voices for their baby; instead, they should maintain a neutral expression and say nothing. On the day I showed up to observe, Philippe was attempting to replicate the Tronick experiment using female lab assistants in place of the mothers. This time I watched from behind a one-way mirror as a young woman and baby engaged each other with smiles and happy voices. Then, on cue, the lab assistant suddenly became motionless and silent. Undeterred, the baby kept smiling and making cooing noises for a while, but her smile soon disappeared when she received no response. Philippe told me his lab assistants had needed intensive training in order to be able to resist the babies' nonverbal attempts to draw them into interactions, and it was easy to see why. Before too long, the baby went back to smiling and making noises again, but not so joyfully this time. Again, the lab assistant resisted the nonverbal pleas to engage, and the baby became still again, looking away.

I was sure this eleven-month-old had given up on trying to make this interaction work, but then she did something extraordinary. She turned her head back, looked earnestly at the lab assistant, raised her hands, put on a dazzling smile, and began to clap hands together to invite the trainee to play patty-cake. I nearly lost it watching this infant's plea to be engaged by this young woman. Fortunately, within a few seconds, another cue was given, and the trainee's face lit up with a wonderful smile. Almost instantly, the infant went from forlorn to joyous again.

As this experiment demonstrates, infants are actively motivated to invite others to interact with them and to do whatever is necessary to sustain that interaction. Even in infancy, before children are able to talk, they will pursue relationships forcefully and use whatever nonverbal tools they have at their disposal to engage with anyone who is present — even a perfect stranger.

Initially, children seek connection as a survival instinct, but this desire for connection doesn't go away once they become old enough to tend to their own needs. The problem is that when these kids get a bit older, these instinctive methods that served them well in infancy are no longer effective or appropriate (imagine if a five-year-old giggled and gurgled to get his mother's attention).

While it is obvious to most how important nonverbal language is in the lives of infants and toddlers who either cannot speak yet or have a limited vocabulary, the exciting things children begin to do with words can quickly overshadow nonverbal communication as a way of connecting. And yet, when it comes to communicating emotions — the very foundation of any relationship — nonverbal language far outweighs verbal language in terms of importance.

As the nonverbal communication expert Albert Mehrabian notes, when emotional messages are transmitted between people, only 7 percent of their meaning is communicated through spoken words, while a full 38 percent is transmitted through tone of voice and 55 percent through body language.[12] Not all researchers agree with these exact percentages, but most support the notion that children need to be proficient in both languages to make relationships work.

HOW NONVERBAL LANGUAGE DEVELOPS

We've all met those enviable individuals who appear to have a gift for drawing people in, who are captivating to listen to, who are enjoyable to be around. These people seem happy, and their cheerfulness rubs off on everyone around them. Although we may not be aware of it at the time, chances are that the reason we respond so positively to these individuals has a lot to do with the warm and inviting expressions on their faces, the way that they modulate their voices to heighten the emotional impact of a story, and how they lean toward us ever so slightly and nod intently when we speak. In so doing, they are letting us know that they see us, they like us, and they want a deeper connection with us, making it exceedingly easy for us to feel the same about them in return. And they do all this without putting it into words.

This is what you want your children to be able to do when they're adults.

Just as basic reading, writing, and arithmetic set the stage for the more complex intellectual and mathematical learning that follows, basic nonverbal skills provide the foundation for the more advanced emotional and social skills children develop later on. So, building a strong foundation in childhood, in other words, paves the way to healthy, fulfilling, and sustainable adult relationships.

With your help, any child can learn the skills they need to become a better nonverbal communicator, and it's possible to start at any age — the younger the better, but it's never too late. If you want to be able to support your child in developing these skills, you need to understand how they are acquired, starting from the earliest stages of development.

Infancy (birth to age two)

The first phase ranges from birth to around two years of age and ends with the introduction of verbal language. In infancy, of course, a child's skills are exclusively nonverbal. And as we have seen, infants are born with a rudimentary set of behaviors that help them obtain the attention and nurturing they crave.

For infants, communication with parents and caregivers is relatively simple: they cry if they are physically uncomfortable or hungry, and you respond to meet these needs. If infants' signals work—that is, if they produce consistent and positive responses from others—then within the first couple of months the infant will begin to perceive that what they do is connected to what happens to them. The awareness that their actions have consequences—positive or negative—provides a foundation for understanding the necessary give-and-take of interpersonal interactions that will become more important as they mature.

As they learn that their actions produce reactions in those around them, infants also begin to sense that they are separate from the faces they see, the voices they hear, and the bodies that inhabit the space around them. With this awareness comes the first inkling of a basic distinction between "self" and "other."

This understanding sets the stage for the first and perhaps most significant relationship we develop in our life, the *attachment relationship*. Although infants show rapid growth physically, cognitively, and emotionally during their first year of life, the attachment between infants and their caregivers is forged entirely through the nonverbal channels of rhythm, facial expressions, tones of voice, personal space, and touch.[13]

Sullivan believed that the reflected appraisals of significant others help infants to know not only that they are separate from others but also whether they are viewed positively or negatively by those others. If infants are surrounded by caregivers who are responsive, smiling, and happy, then chances are their early self-concept will be positive. But if those caring for infants are consistently sad, angry, or anxious and reject the infants' pleas for attention, those infants are likely to develop negative self-concepts.

Initially, infants use all their innate and early nonverbal abilities to bond with the caregivers who provide them with what they need physically to live. But by age two, infants will have experienced a wealth of social interactions and developed a richer nonverbal vocabulary as a result. Most adults will continue to use words when interacting with them, but it will still be the vocal inflection, intensity, volume, and rhythm of those words that carry the communicative weight.

Early Childhood Phase (ages two to four)

There are three major developments happening in the early childhood phase, which begins at age two. The first is that verbal language arrives on the scene, combining with existing nonverbal language to create new ways of understanding and relating to the social world. Second is that children begin to become consciously aware of the nonverbal messages they are sending and receiving. And third is that their world expands, particularly as they start preschool—and the opportunities for nonverbal learning expand with it.

At the start of this phase, you may be a bit torn between wanting to encourage the learning of new words and not wanting to abandon the tried-and-true baby talk and nonverbal language you have shared with your children for the past couple of years. I can relate. When my son didn't like something as a little boy, he called it "chicky." Such invented words that we had used together felt like keepsakes for me — almost like our own secret code — and I found them difficult to give up. But actual words soon won out because they offered a vehicle for communication that could be understood beyond the family circle.

As the parent of a young child, you've probably spent a great deal of time and effort in shaping your child's verbal language by repeating correct pronunciations of words, restating sentences using the proper grammar, and reducing the amount of baby talk that was so prevalent in infancy. Parents are understandably proud when a child starts using new, more advanced words and may even be embarrassed if children are slow to pick up on this new way of communicating.

But more sophisticated forms of nonverbal communication are being learned during this phase as well. Maturation of the brain and nervous system allows children to process and send more subtle signals in all the nonverbal channels. At this age, your child can likely make a "mad" face on cue and sense when you are angry or happy based on your facial expressions and tone of voice. At the same time, he is gaining more awareness of the messages he is sending and receiving via other nonverbal channels; for example, he may be starting to understand that a hug means affection and may be learning to mimic parents' rhythms.

Needless to say, nonverbal communication often gets neglected once a child starts "talking." As parents we're often so excited about words that we don't pay as much attention to the nonverbal messages our kids are sending, and we become less attuned to them as a result. At the point your child knows how to ask for a hug using words, you might miss the nonverbal signs that he is looking forlorn and in need of a cuddle if he isn't verbally asking for one.

During this phase, kids also become social. As a parent, you'll doubtless find yourself setting up playdates, during which your child's nonverbal skills are being expanded as he interacts with peers and adults from outside the family circle. Playdates also offer children the opportunity to observe a broader range of interactions, such as conversations between adults. Through these experiences, they gain access to a richer variety of facial expressions, tone of voice, space usage, and other nonverbal information than was modeled in their immediate family. If all goes as planned, children will learn the basics of social interaction, both through play and through the corrections to social behavior made by watchful parents, caregivers, and teachers. These skills become the foundation for the next phase, when he will have to navigate these interactions without as much help in full-time school. You can think of this phase as a kind of controlled rehearsal for the relationships that will be built in late childhood.

Late Childhood Phase (ages five to ten)

Up to this point, parents and caregivers have been a child's main source of information and knowledge about how to relate to others. But in late childhood, when formal schooling begins, the training wheels come off, and children must now learn how to relate to their peers without so much direction. Now it's time for them to test what they've learned and rehearsed in the prior phase.

Learning these new sets of interpersonal skills without supervision and guidance can be incredibly difficult. Suddenly, children are surrounded by a whole new set of nonverbal vocabularies—many of which will inevitably differ from the ones they've encountered at home. For example, children from homes where gesticulations are intense and where voices are loud may miss the more subtle messages of peers and teachers. Or it could be that children from families that rarely exhibit strong displays of emotion may be terrified of loud voices on the playground, mistaking their peers' playful yelling for anger. Learning to interpret these messages correctly is a process of trial and error, and it is inevitable that errors will occur.

If children are able to successfully navigate their way through this maze, they are likely to form a unique and wonderful relationship: a best friend. Arguably the most significant milestone of the late childhood phase, this usually happens around the age of ten or eleven and is usually, but not exclusively, an intense same-sex friendship in which issues of trust and caring can be explored and resolved, giving each child insight into who they are and how they relate to others.

Once these "chums"—as Sullivan called them—pair up, they tend to splinter off from the larger social group and spend an inordinate amount of time with each other, exploring shared interests, discussing classmates and the adults in their lives, and often divulging their innermost thoughts and secrets. What makes this friendship so important is that the two children—consciously or not—come to rely on each other for feedback about how they behave interpersonally. Sullivan called this process "consensual validation" because both individuals become more aware of their own behavior through the process of communicating freely with another human being. Chums provide each other not only with valuable opportunities to practice social interactions and social behavior but also with valuable information about what they might be doing right or wrong in those interactions. Another characteristic of this unique relationship, according to Sullivan, is that it may be the first time children voluntarily put the needs and wants of others ahead of their own. These experiences will become invaluable when children enter adolescence and begin to pursue more complex friendships as well as romantic and/or sexual relationships.

THE ANATOMY OF A RELATIONSHIP: THE FOUR-PHASE MODEL

As we've seen, when your child is younger, you as a parent have a lot of control over his social life, selecting whom he should interact with, the length of the interaction, and where the interaction takes place. That changes when your child reaches school age. Suddenly, these decisions—with whom to be friends, how much time to spend with a friend, and how to spend that time together—are made largely on his own (though teachers may also play an important role). School is a place where children can begin to form rewarding friendships, but it is also a place where children can experience rejection and isolation, often because of nonverbal messages they are unwittingly sending and erroneously reading.

From the late childhood phase on, any friendship a child forms follows a pattern. And this sequence, which my colleague Marshall Duke and I first codified back in the 1980s, provides a template for the relationships those children will form as adults: children *choose* a likely candidate for friendship, they *initiate* the relationship, they *deepen* the relationship, and lastly, they go through a relationship *transition* when the social occasion, school day / week / semester / year ends. Each of these phases of the relationship requires the use of nonverbal and verbal language skills — but some skills play a more important role in certain phases than in others. Understanding the patterns by which late childhood friendships form and develop can help you identify where your child is doing well and where he may need to learn more in order to connect meaningfully with others.[14]

1. Choosing

The choice phase is where every relationship begins. Research shows that a child's decision about whom he's going to befriend usually takes place in a matter of seconds. This means that children are using information gathered from nonverbal cues in clothing, facial expressions, and posture to decide to approach another child.

Ideally, when parents of very young children make these choices for them, they will share the reasons for their choices with their children. For example, when inviting a child for a playdate, the parent could say something like, "I think you are going to have a good time with Ravi. She always listens to me and shares her playthings with you." Not only does this sharing of information help children understand their parents' choices, but it also tells the children what is expected of them.

By the time your child reaches school age, then, he should already have some sense of how to choose a friend. You can imagine him faced with a schoolyard filled with children he doesn't know on the first day of school. He wants to find someone to play with. Over to his left, a few boys are playing ball and a ball comes loose and rolls toward him. A boy in a Green Bay Packers cap runs after the ball, picks it up, and smiles. In that friendly smile, your child senses an invitation. He smiles back and begins walking toward the boy wearing the Packers cap. He has chosen to make a new friend.

2. Initiating

The initiation phase is what happens next. Your child follows his new friend as he joins the three other boys playing ball. He waits until there's a break in what is going on. "Hi," he says with a smile. "Can I join in?" The other boys introduce themselves quickly and your child says, "I'm a Packer Backer too. I've got a Packers cap at home. I'll wear it tomorrow."

The boy with the Packers cap says, "Remember when they won that game when it was a million degrees below zero?" Your child excitedly comments about how the field was like ice, and soon there are five boys happily playing.

For a five-year-old meeting new peers for the first time on a playground, even a seemingly simple interaction like this one is a difficult task involving both nonverbal and verbal behaviors: Your child waited patiently and, sensing the rhythm of the game, chose the right moment to cut in. He didn't intrude on their game, showing his respect for their personal space. When he did introduce himself, he smiled warmly and made eye contact. Then he made "small talk" before he asked to join in. I think we all can imagine many ways that the interaction could have gone much less successfully than it did.

The initiation phase is when the real give-and-take of social information through nonverbal and verbal channels gets under way. Your child is in uncharted relationship waters now. For the first time, he is running his own show and it is up to him to get this potential relationship off to a successful start.

3. Deepening

Over time, if all goes well, your child's friendships will deepen in ways that would have been all but impossible in the earlier phases of development, in which friendships are usually fleeting and revolve around a shared activity. Hallmarks of a deepening relationship include trust, self-disclosure, acceptance, and mutual understanding. As C. S. Lewis put it: Friendship is born at that moment when one person says to another, "What! You too? I thought I was the only one."

The process of deepening a friendship involves a lot of give-and-take, much of it nonverbal; when one person speaks, the other responds not only through their words but through facial expressions, body language, and tone of voice as well. Your child will disclose something about himself, then look to his friend to gauge the reaction. If the friend nods, smiles, or makes encouraging gestures, your child will know to keep going. As children spend more and more time together, they become increasingly attuned to the nonverbal cues that communicate what the other is thinking or feeling. They begin to inhabit the same physical space and share the same rhythms and can often be seen hugging or walking arm in arm, with smiles on their faces.

4. Transitioning

While deepening a relationship can be hard work for some kids, virtually all children will struggle with handling relationship transitions positively. In late childhood, these transitions happen more often than you may be aware: at the end of the school day, or a playdate, for example. Sometimes the transition is more intense, such as the end of the school year or the Little League season or the last day of camp. Other times a transition in a friendship happens when a child has to move to a new town or school. And of course, there are times when one or both children actively decide not to continue the friendship, whether it's over some fight or disagreement or the friendship simply having run its course.

Although transitions can sometimes be painful, it's important to remember that each transition can also be a new beginning. Even as adults, transitions can make us uncomfortable, so we often rush through them as quickly as possible, without considering the unique information the experience can offer us.

Picture two ten-year-old girls, Gina and Ilana, on the last day of school. These friends sat next to each other during class for the whole school year because their last names both begin with *M*. While not "best-best friends," their bond has deepened over the course of the school year and they are sad they probably won't see much of each other over the summer. As they clean out their desks, they talk about the past school year. They remember how they were so shy with each other at first. They reminisce about the science fair, field day, and other memorable events leading up to this the final day of school. Not all the times were fun, though, they admit. There were disagreements, and they both remember a particularly bad one during field day, when Ilana didn't choose Gina for her team.

When their desks are cleaned out and have passed the teacher's inspection, it's time to leave. Each girl reaches sheepishly into her book bag and retrieves the present that they bought for the other. They hold hands as they walk out to their separate school buses. It's time to part ways. Usually, their exchanges with each other are lively, but today they are much quieter and more subdued, which makes their goodbye hugs more meaningful. In hushed tones, they tell each other to have a good summer. Transitioning is the point in the life of a relationship when you can help your child look back and see discernable patterns in how the relationship developed. Reflecting how she chose, began, and deepened her ties with another person can yield valuable lessons that can be applied to the next set of relationships. And the more complex and important the relationship, the more she can learn from it.

· · · · · ·

AS WE'VE SEEN, nonverbal communication plays a key role in the development of close friendships at every stage in a child's life. What this means is that if your child is struggling socially, the best thing you can do to support him is help him acquire the necessary nonverbal language. The methods for doing so, as I will show in the following chapters, are simple and straightforward. But first, we need to understand exactly what these critical nonverbal skills are and why they often take a back seat to verbal language learning.

CHAPTER 2

The Six Types of Nonverbal Communication

A Primer

ALTHOUGH EVERYONE USES NONVERBAL LANGUAGE IN DAY-to-day life, not many of us spend much time thinking about how and why we use it. As with any language, fluency requires the ability to express yourself clearly, understand what others are saying, and determine the most appropriate way to express something in any given situation or setting. The difference is that unlike verbal language, much of this kind of communication happens unconsciously, and as a result, we tend to ignore it or take it for granted. In fact, nonverbal communication falls into six main categories that I will delve into in much greater detail in chapters to come. For now, a primer:

1. **Rhythm:** The pace at which we respond to others, both with our physical gestures and within the interplay of conversation.

   Rhythm underpins all of our interactions with others. When you wait for someone else to speak rather than cutting in or when you extend a hand to shake almost at the same moment another person extends a hand, you are instinctively using rhythm to convey respect and make others feel comfortable around you. We've all had the experience of having a conversation with someone and the interaction just flows. This means you and the other person share a compatible rhythm.

   On the other hand, when someone doesn't wait for his turn to speak and talks over you, it can come across as rude or awkward. Or if you begin a conversation with someone and she pauses for a few too many beats before replying to your questions, speaks too quickly, or answers with only a few words, it can throw your own rhythm off-kilter. In other words, when rhythm is incompatible, it can lead to extremely awkward social interactions.

2. **Facial expressions:** The way we use our eyes, mouth, eyebrows, and forehead to communicate emotion.

   Your facial expressions allow you to reveal what you are thinking or feeling without saying a word. When you look enthusiastic, others respond with their own enthusiasm. When you look unhappy, others will check to make sure that you're okay.

During the pandemic, we all learned how difficult it was to communicate while wearing masks that obscured much of our faces. Conversations became drained of life — and it took a much greater effort to get our message across using our words and eyes alone.[1]

3. **Personal space:** The area surrounding us that we don't wish others to broach (unless we invite them).

Imagine someone you don't know standing too close to you at a party. You feel that a physical boundary has been violated and may step away. Most of us are instinctively aware of others' personal space and become uncomfortable when strangers move into what we consider our personal zone.

In the throes of the pandemic, we all became much more aware of personal space and became accustomed to putting an even greater distance between ourselves and others — a habit that still lingers. When we give someone else the correct amount of personal space, we are being responsive to their needs without saying a word, making others automatically feel more at ease around us.[2]

4. **Physical touch:** When we come so close to others that physical contact takes place, either intentionally or unintentionally.

When it is appropriate, physical touch can be one of the most effective ways to communicate the warmth you feel toward another person. As a parent, you will often use touch to soothe your child and to allay her fears with an affectionate hug or squeeze of a hand. But touch can also be problematic. Until you have reached a point of familiarity and intimacy with someone in which touch becomes consensual and appropriate, physical contact can be seen as an invasion of the other person's bodily autonomy. This is true even when the "touching" is accidental because the person being touched may not know the "intent" of the toucher.

When someone touches you — whether it's a pat on the back, an arm around your shoulders, or a hug — before that point of intimacy has been reached, it can be extremely disconcerting, even when the touching is accidental. Even shaking hands — a formalized way of touching others — and hugging can often go wrong. Most of us have probably experienced the classic gaffe of misreading the degree of friendship and going in for a hug while the other person may be initiating a handshake.

5. **Vocalics:** All the vocal communications we use that don't include words, including the pitch, volume, and speed of our speech; our hesitations; and sounds such as ums and ahs.

We all know what it's like to converse with someone who talks too fast or too slowly, and at too low or high a volume. Trying to keep up a conversation with someone who mumbles or speaks so softly that we have to strain our ears to understand them or who peppers her sentences with too many ums and ahs can be exhausting. And when someone talks a mile a minute or at the top of their lungs, it can quickly make us feel as if we need a break from listening to the person. On the other hand, when someone speaks to us at a comfortable volume and pitch, when making out their words doesn't demand all our mental energy, we can pay more attention to the meaning behind what they are saying, and we tend to respond more positively to them as a result.

6. **Body language:** The movements we make with parts of our bodies, especially our hands, to communicate or emphasize something. Body language also includes our posture, as well as the things we put on our bodies to convey emotion or status, including clothes, jewelry, scents, makeup, and tattoos.

People who use their hands to express how they are feeling—or to drive home a point—generally tend to be more engaging conversationalists and speakers.[3] To some degree this is true because gestures help emphasize what's being said and drive the interaction along, making the speaker come across as open, friendly, and engaged. Conversely, when someone stands with their arms stiff at their sides or folded tightly across their chest and never uses their hands to gesticulate while speaking, it can give the impression that the person is ill at ease—and can even feel slightly off-putting and cold emotionally.

Posture is another important aspect of body language and is the only nonverbal signal we can pick up from a distance. People who stand up straight, with their arms loosely at their sides, rather than clasped in front of their body, will instantly seem more confident and relaxed, even from many yards away, and instinctively, we are more likely to respond positively to that person.[4] On the other hand, think of a classroom of teenagers slumped in their chairs. They might not all be feeling disinterested, but their body language is sending a powerful message that they are bored and eager to leave.

Objectics are the items we wear on our bodies, and they can convey strong messages to others about who we are—our tastes and preferences, our moods, and even the groups or subcultures with whom we identify. Showing up for a job interview in business-appropriate attire, for example, can send a very different message than going to a rock concert in a leather jacket and a lot of metal jewelry, but in both cases, we're signaling something about how we wish to be perceived. For children, too, objectics are a way to identify peers who may share their interests or a group they think they may fit in with. But they can also make a child feel excluded or have a distancing effect.

A TALE OF TWO LANGUAGES: SIMILARITIES AND DIFFERENCES

Now that we've looked at the different types of nonverbal language, it's important to understand the ways that verbal and nonverbal languages—our two major modes of communication—are alike and, most importantly, how they differ.

THE SIX TYPES OF NONVERBAL COMMUNICATION

Verbal and nonverbal language share at least four major characteristics.

1. They are both learned.

As with verbal language, nonverbal language is something that babies begin to acquire from the moment they open their eyes—and they continue to acquire it with each year that goes by. For both languages, the process of learning follows a typical sequence, and both sequences possess their own developmental milestones that reflect a child's progress.

Up to about the first year, most of a child's milestones are nonverbal—for example, smiling, pointing, waving bye-bye. Your child learns that nodding means yes, and a shaking head means no. She realizes that someone who is happy may smile at her and use an encouraging tone of voice or give a thumbs-up. She comes to understand that when someone is upset with her, that person may frown at her. After the year mark, verbal milestones predominate: the first word, the first sentence, the first time the child asks for something by name. Over time the child's vocabulary grows, as does her ability to construct more complex sentences and, eventually, to read. Meanwhile, her nonverbal vocabulary continues to develop as well, even if we don't mark those milestones with the same fanfare as we do verbal ones.

It follows that because nonverbal communication is learned, it can also be taught. In the same way that we might correct a child who mispronounces a word, we can also correct a child who is speaking too loudly, who is interrupting a sibling, or who bumps into a playmate.

2. They are both richly complex.

The main component of verbal language is, of course, words. And the English language has plenty of them. In fact, it is one of the world's richest languages, with 171,476 entries in the *Oxford English Dictionary*, second edition. But nonverbal language is also rich in complexity. According to one influential theorist of nonverbal communication, Ray Birdwhistell, literally thousands of different cues can be discerned from human movement, or what he called "kinesics."[5] And renowned linguist Mario Pei went even further when he estimated that humans can produce an astounding seven hundred thousand or more physical signals that function as nonverbal communicative cues.[6]

This makes sense when you think about how many different emotional cues can be sent nonverbally: happiness, sadness, anger, fear, disgust, surprise, to name just a few. Then think about how those cues can vary in intensity: high versus low and everywhere in between. Not only that, but these emotional cues can be carried simultaneously on different nonverbal channels: via our faces, voices, gestures, posture. Mastering and making sense of the constantly changing kaleidoscope of nonverbal cues is no small task indeed and is just as crucial to a child's social and academic success as the mastery of verbal language.

3. **They are both composed of abilities to understand and express.**

Chances are, you've given a lot of thought to your child's competence in reading, writing, spelling, and speaking. Verbal skills can be separated into those we learn to *understand* the written and spoken words of others and those we use to *express ourselves in words* to others.

But like most parents, you've probably spent much less time focusing on how well your child is doing nonverbally. Nonverbal language skills can be classified in the exact same way that verbal ones can: as "expressive" (the ability to use nonverbal cues to express oneself) or "receptive" (the ability to read nonverbal cues). As is also the case for verbal language, the ability to *read* nonverbal cues is separate and independent from the skill in *expressing* them. So in the same way that a child might struggle with reading comprehension but have no trouble constructing a complex sentence, for example, a child can be adept at reading others' facial expressions but still struggle with expressing their own. Another child might be quite skilled at expressing their own emotions nonverbally but be less advanced when it comes to reading and understanding the emotional information being conveyed by the facial expressions, tones of voice, and gestures of their peers. Both types of skills are important. After all, it doesn't matter if you know how to behave in response to an angry person if you misread his or her angry facial expression as sad.

The good news is that just because a child is having trouble interpreting nonverbal cues doesn't necessarily mean she is having any difficulty using them. And most children are perfectly capable of learning both receptive and expressive nonverbal skills but for a variety of reasons may not have had the opportunities to acquire the appropriate competencies for their age and situation.

4. They are both shaped by culture.

Each culture has its own nonverbal language, just as it has its own verbal language. Consider the traditional ways Americans and Japanese people greet one another. In Japan the custom is to bow, but even if someone uses the Western practice of shaking hands, the grip is light and the eyes are averted. Contrast that with the somewhat aggressive American practice of beginning the greeting with a firm handshake and direct eye-contact.

I have a colleague, world-famous primatologist Frans de Waal, who is multilingual and one of the few members of our faculty who can present his research in verbal languages other than English. I've had the opportunity to observe Frans when he is speaking to someone in a language other than English, and it has helped to remind me that each verbal language is accompanied by its own nonverbal one. When Frans speaks Dutch or German, for example, I notice his posture is more erect and he uses fewer gestures than when he speaks Italian or French. Unlike Frans, most people who learn a foreign language never learn to use the accompanying nonverbal language. They may be bilingual, but they are "uni-kinesic," meaning they use only their native nonverbal language. Frans, on the other hand, would be described as multilingual *and* multi-kinesic.

Despite all their similarities, *verbal and nonverbal language also differ in multiple ways*—and these differences are key to understanding why children who lag behind in these skills find themselves struggling, both emotionally and socially.

1. **We are less conscious of how we use nonverbal language compared to verbal language.**
While we are generally very conscious of what we are saying or writing, rarely do we have the same level of awareness about how we are expressing ourselves nonverbally—or how we are interpreting the nonverbal signals we receive from others. This is why some children (like Jack, whom we met earlier), are unaware not only of their own nonverbal missteps but also of how others are reacting to those missteps, and why. It's also why problems with nonverbal language seem harder to diagnose than those with verbal language.

Complicating matters further, most people aren't always aware of why they react to these missteps the way they do. We might feel frustrated after conversing with someone who peppers their speech with excessively long pauses but unable to identify the source of the frustration. Even on the rare occasions where we might be aware of and able to articulate the nonverbal missteps of others, our good manners may prevent us from pointing them out. For example, if someone stands too close to us or stares at us for too long, it's likely that we will simply move away from that person rather than telling them we feel uncomfortable.

As a result, when kids make nonverbal mistakes, they rarely get the corrective feedback they need. Rather, they may be able to sense something is off in their attempts to connect, but they don't know what it is or how to make things better. If they continue to pursue a connection while still making mistakes that make other children uncomfortable, they could end up being socially excluded, labeled an "oddball," or worse.

This lack of awareness about how emotions are transmitted through nonverbal channels may contribute to the development of failed social adjustments and emotional problems, especially during the transition from childhood to adolescence. And in the absence of any intervention, this low emotional awareness may pave the way for more serious difficulties down the line.

2. **Nonverbal language is used more continuously and involuntarily than verbal language and is impossible to turn off.**

Nonverbal behavior is always on. It's on when we speak and when we are quiet, with or without our permission. Think of how, even once you've finished talking, your body remains in constant motion, sending signals with your posture, gestures, and facial expressions. When I give talks, I often mention this characteristic of nonverbal language, saying, "I'm the only person talking at the moment, but each and every one of you is communicating with me now by the way you are sitting or stretching or rolling your eyes, or yawning or looking around the room. You can't stop it and I can't help but be affected by it." As soon as I say this, something unique happens to the people in the audience: they freeze. Everyone sits up straight, trying not to move a muscle, which means that any movement they do make is made much louder by the effort. I usually hear squeaking noises coming from desks or chairs as people try their hardest not to communicate in the ways I've just described but do, in spite of themselves.

Paul Watzlawick, world-famous psychotherapist, suggested that we cannot *not* communicate nonverbally![7] When we consider the involuntary nature of nonverbal communication coupled with the fact that it often takes place outside our awareness, it is easy to see how children could be continually making nonverbal mistakes without realizing it.

3. Nonverbal language is learned less directly and less systematically compared to verbal language.

At school, children are taught to use verbal and written language in formalized, intentional ways. Spelling tests and written homework assignments are corrected, marked, and returned to students, who may then be told to redo the portions of the assignment that they answered incorrectly. And when the children read out loud, teachers will correct students' pronunciation, grammar, and other errors. No one ever questions why things are done this way; we accept that learning to read and write is a critical component of a child's formal education.

In contrast, educators rarely dedicate classroom time to teaching *nonverbal* language. Your child won't be graded on an assignment that asks him to identify the correct facial expression for "sadness" so he can learn how it differs from "anger." There certainly won't be quizzes about how close to stand next to peers, how long to maintain eye contact when answering the teacher's question, or how to use body language to show interest in what a classmate is saying.

These skills are just as important as knowing when to use a semicolon in a sentence, yet they are rarely on the curriculum.

4. Nonverbal language has a more visceral impact than verbal language.

When someone breaks a rule of verbal language—a spelling error in an email or using a figure of speech incorrectly, for example—we usually shrug it off. That's because we process the mistake intellectually, often (correctly) attributing it to mere carelessness. But when people fail to follow the rules of nonverbal language—perhaps a stranger sits down next to you in a movie theater despite there being plenty of empty seats with equally good views of the screen—you process it emotionally and are likely to respond intuitively, perhaps by scooting away from the person, whom you now view as strange or even threatening.

5. When nonverbal and verbal language convey conflicting emotional messages, we tend to accept the nonverbal one as true.

THE SIX TYPES OF NONVERBAL COMMUNICATION

Despite the fact that nonverbal communication flies under the radar, it's actually extremely powerful, often more powerful than verbal communication. When you ask someone if she is having a good day, and she says yes in a sad, shaky voice, you're likely to believe what's being conveyed by her tone rather than her words. Similarly, if the person you're chatting with at a party keeps telling you how much they are enjoying the conversation but steals glances at his watch or phone every thirty seconds, his nonverbal behavior is sending a clear message that he'd rather be someplace else. Incongruence between the verbal and nonverbal can cause countless problems for a child who is unaware of the overpowering emotional messages he may be sending to others.

* * * * * *

AS WE'VE SEEN, nonverbal language is every bit as complex, and every bit as useful, in communicating information and emotion as its verbal partner. In the chapters ahead, you'll learn the rules and dynamics of nonverbal language—and how to help your child master them.

PART 2

THE SILENT ORCHESTRA

Unlocking the Power of Nonverbal Language (to Play the Beautiful Music of Relationships)

I T WAS TEN A.M. AND I WAS STANDING BEHIND A PODIUM HIGH ON A stage looking down at an audience that included teachers, speech therapists, psychologists, psychiatrists, and other professionals, but most importantly, parents. I had been asked to be the keynote speaker at this conference at the University of California, Davis, on the social adjustment of children. Perched up onstage, I couldn't help but feel uncomfortable. Not only was I far away from the audience, but most of my body was hidden behind the wooden podium. Here I was, coming to speak about the importance of nonverbal communication, and the audience couldn't see my nonverbals—and I couldn't see theirs. So, I turned to the person in charge of technical matters and asked for a portable microphone, attached it to my lapel, and walked down the stairs until I reached the level where the participants were seated. At closer proximity, I could more effectively use my nonverbal language to communicate my message and pick up nonverbal cues from my audience at the same time.

To be sure I could connect with as many people as possible, I walked from one side of the auditorium to the other and from the front to the very back, as I described each of the nonverbal social communication channels and how it affects the relationship process. The components of nonverbal language, I explained as I moved around the room, are a lot like musicians in an orchestra. Just as the individual musicians have to master their instrument and play with the right beat and intensity in total synchronicity with those around them, so, too, must each nonverbal component work in concert with the others to convey a rich and resonant message.

Like musicians practicing, children need to practice each of the nonverbal instruments until they master it and can sustain their performance throughout the phases of their relationships: choosing, initiating, deepening, and transitioning. In the same way that practice gets harder for musicians as the pieces of music they attempt increase in complexity, children need to be ready to play their nonverbal instruments with even greater facility as they face the increasing social complexities that come with age. My goal over the next chapters is to introduce you to all the instruments in the orchestra of nonverbal communication, so you can help guide children as they develop these essential skills.

Each chapter introduces a specific nonverbal communication channel, its origins, how it's learned, and how its importance may change with age. Each chapter also describes the impact of that channel on the development of children's friendships, along with how to gauge children's current skill levels and suggestions for how to help your child improve them. Although readers may choose to flip to a chapter on any specific nonverbal channel of interest, I must emphasize that none work alone; again, like instruments in an orchestra, each works in harmony with the others.

CHAPTER 3

Rhythm

The Stealth Nonverbal Channel

I FIRST ENCOUNTERED EIGHT-YEAR-OLD ISOBEL WHEN I WAS ASKED to observe her within her third-grade class at a small school in a southern city of Georgia. Isobel's teachers were concerned about her disruptive behavior and had even suggested a variety of possible diagnoses to her parents, including ADHD and even autism spectrum disorder. This is why I had been asked to visit and make an assessment.

In this particular elementary school, students changed classes twice a day, to prepare them for the more frequent classroom transitions that they would experience later in middle school and to give them some relief from sitting in the same room for prolonged periods of time. When the school bell rang to indicate the end of class, I watched as the children got ready to spill out into the hall. While other students quickly put their notebooks away and stood behind their desks, waiting to be dismissed, Isobel dawdled until she was the last student to stand by her desk and the last to file out of the room. Out in the hallway, however, Isobel walked faster than the other children, pushing ahead of the first four students in front of her. When teachers called out, "Isobel, stay in line!" the little girl stopped and returned to where she originally was supposed to be, but then began to walk slower than the students ahead of and behind her, resulting in a human traffic jam.

In the next classroom, Isobel continued to be out of step with her peers. Although academically capable, she rarely followed group directions unless her name was called specifically, and even then, the directions had to be repeated especially for her. Isobel wasn't belligerent or uncooperative; she just seemed to be clueless about when she should or shouldn't be doing something. For example, when the class was called to the story rug, she moved slowly and was the last to get there, inevitably stepping on the hand of someone who was already seated as she wedged herself into the circle.

Out on the playground, Isobel tried to join the games or activities that were already under way, but because she consistently joined late, she found herself left out. She really wanted to be included but seemed unaware that her timing was creating problems. When Isobel did manage to join an activity, she seemed to do well enough—on the whole, the other children accepted her, but they often showed signs of annoyance at the interruptions and delays she caused.

RHYTHM

After observing Isobel in class and at recess, I met with her one-on-one and administered a series of tests. In one assessment, I pulled out two sets of rhythm sticks, handed one to Isobel, and asked her to play them in sync with me. She couldn't; sometimes I could hear her sticks click ahead of mine, and sometimes they clicked well after mine. After finishing the tests and reading her complete file, I felt certain I had uncovered Isobel's problem: she was struggling with the nonverbal channel of rhythm. This was why she had so much difficulty matching her pace to that of the students around her; she simply wasn't picking up the "beat" of the classroom. But the more important finding was this: as obvious as her rhythm difficulties were to me, Isobel seemed entirely unaware of her mistakes.

All children need to learn to get in sync with the rhythm of the classroom and of their peers in order to thrive in the school setting. However, because this—like all other forms of nonverbal communication—is learned indirectly, not all children will pick it up at the same pace. For some children, moving in step with the rest of the class can be challenging. Even those with a natural facility for rhythm may be thrown off by whatever might be happening in their lives, much like a metronome knocked from its perch on the piano.[1]

Much of my school consulting time is spent watching for the children who are "out of rhythm" with their peers, because inevitably these are the students having difficulties with social situations as well. They tend to fail at the turn-taking necessary for successful social harmony. Because they don't know when to stop talking and listen, their conversations and interactions quickly deteriorate. They finish eating lunch too soon or too late; when they finish too early, they are likely to initiate interactions that annoy their peers who are still eating, and if they are still eating while everyone else is done, they miss out on the post-lunch socializing that is so important to the development of peer friendship. Transitions from one activity to the next and traveling from one class to another are challenging for them. They are the ones still pasting objects on poster board for an art project while everyone else has finished, has cleaned up, and is ready to move on. Imagine how a child who is moving too fast or too slow could frustrate a teacher who is trying to deal with twenty to thirty children at the same time, leading that teacher to speak sharply to or discipline the out-of-step student. In turn, the child might withdraw and lose confidence, still unaware of what she is doing wrong.

A big part of any teacher's job is to set the rhythm necessary for healthy social interaction and learning, especially in elementary school. Before the pandemic short-circuited in-person education, most elementary school teachers probably had to deal with one or two children like Isobel in their classrooms, but after many months of remote learning, the numbers of "Isobels" returning to in-person class increased exponentially. Children who were already struggling with rhythm found themselves even farther behind their peers, and those who might have had no trouble with rhythm before the pandemic were now out of practice.

While it's true that many children who struggled with rhythm in their interactions were given a break from those challenges because they were home—which some parents saw as a positive effect of the school shutdown—without opportunities for learning experiences, these children's shortcomings had only worsened by the time they returned to more complex face-to-face interactions with peers and teachers in school. The end result was chaotic classrooms in which teachers had to work that much harder to bring students back in sync with one another.

The truth is all of us may have become "rhythm lazy" due to the excessive amount of time we've spent interacting via screens, and this was true long before the pandemic. Yet it's undeniable that Zoom schooling has seriously disrupted our children's ability to use rhythm appropriately in social situations. While our children were learning online via screens, the rhythm of their interactions changed dramatically.[2] Zoom, FaceTime, and other video meeting platforms have delays and silences that don't happen in person—after all, in real-life conversation, no one has to pause to unmute themselves before speaking! Online, we have to adjust our natural conversational back-and-forth, and it's much harder to get into a flow. Whereas during in-person interactions, we are constantly picking up on nuances of speech and movement, staying alert to the rhythms of others and adapting our own rhythms and movements to match and stay in sync, during virtual interactions, we simply aren't required to pay attention in the same way. As one of my students shared with me during an in-person class discussion: "To be honest I really like Zoom classes because I can get away with so many things I could never dream of attempting to get away with in person."

Although a child's struggles with rhythm may create disruptions in classrooms and social problems for that child when interacting with peers, the good news is that rhythm, like all nonverbal skills, can be taught. And as rhythm plays a central role in the other nonverbal channels, when rhythm skills are improved, the child will likely see gains in the various other skills necessary for making relationships work out well. In the orchestra of nonverbal communication, rhythm is like the conductor, helping all the other instruments stay in sync. Fortunately, there is plenty we can all do to help support our children in acquiring and improving this vital nonverbal skill. That's what this chapter is going to help you to do.

WHY RHYTHM MATTERS

You may be surprised that I'm devoting this first chapter to the subject of rhythm. If I asked you to name the most important form of nonverbal communication, I'm guessing you would likely say "body language" or "facial expressions." But in fact, rhythm has more far-reaching implications for our social interactions than any of the other nonverbal channels, because it is at once the most ubiquitous and the (arguably) least recognized and least appreciated of the nonverbal skills.

It's impossible to overstate all the ways in which rhythm—defined as a strong, regular, repeated pattern of movement or sound—permeates our lives.[3] The renowned poet Maya Angelou reportedly once said that "everything in the universe has rhythm, everything dances," and she's right; rhythms are embedded in so many aspects of our lives that we tend to notice only once they're disrupted. We sleep and wake to the rhythm of the sun rising and setting. We dress to the rhythm of changing temperature and seasons. We drive our kids to school and catch the bus or train to work and have our first cup of coffee at pretty much the same time every day.

Beyond the rhythms of our daily routines, we are each born with different temperaments, or a genetically determined rhythm of our emotional responses to our world. The sun will come up at the same time for all of us, but while some of us wake up exhilarated and ready to face the day, others pull the sheets over their heads and go back to sleep. Some of us are temperamentally calm, with moods like a steady drumbeat, while others' moods are more volatile, like a drumbeat punctuated by loud clangs of the cymbal. And we develop these temperaments at a very young age; if you walk into a preschool classroom, you will immediately observe that some kids are quicker to engage and more high-energy than others, while some tend to be cautious, shy, and slower to warm up. Humans, in other words, are creatures of rhythm.[4]

These physical and biological rhythms often go unnoticed, and yet they are deeply ingrained in us; so much so that we may find it hard to modulate our natural rhythms to accommodate others.[5] Those who prefer to be solitary are likely to have a harder time syncing up with the rhythm of the office—especially when thrust into the company of coworkers on a Monday morning after a quiet weekend at home. And those who are outgoing and energetic might struggle to slow down to match the rhythm of someone who is temperamentally more reserved.

When we're not in sync with someone else's rhythm, we tend to react negatively, even if we don't realize the cause of our discomfort. For example, if you have been at the office all day and are hyperfocused on a project with a tight deadline, you may find it tough to switch out of your "work rhythm," and into the more laid-back "home rhythm" that your spouse settled into upon returning from his own workplace a few hours earlier. You might get frustrated with your spouse as a result, and he may get frustrated with you in return. And when slow talkers and fast talkers get together, their rhythms may be out of sync, and as a result, communication can misfire.

Rhythm affects the impact of our verbal language too. If we wish to effectively communicate our excitement, we generally speed up our words and our gestures become more exaggerated. If, on the other hand, we tell someone we're excited but slowly, without any gestures at all, our message becomes confusing and difficult to understand.

But when we *are* in sync with others, it improves our interactions dramatically, in part by helping to bring many of the other nonverbal channels into alignment. When we go for a walk with a friend, for example, we expect that person to match our rhythm by walking alongside us rather than behind or in front of us. If we slow, they slow. If we speed up, so do they. In this scenario, their posture and gestures, the tone and volume of their voice, and even their facial expressions often sync up with ours.

To be in rhythm with one another while walking is a marker of being in a shared relationship, and the better we know someone, the better the chance our rhythms will match without much conscious awareness, whereas when we walk with someone we've just met, we may not fall into lockstep quite as easily.

Such subtle but crucial interpersonal rhythms are initially learned within our families and then are modified through interactions at school, during extracurricular activities, or by spending time with other friends and relatives. By interacting with individuals whose rhythms vary in pace, tempo, and pattern of speech and movement, children learn how to accommodate and adjust to a broader range of rhythms and develop more sophisticated rhythms of their own.

Because of the fundamental role rhythm plays in our relationships, lack of rhythm ability is usually a reliable marker of social problems in children. Relationships are all about connections, but to make successful connections, children need to be in step with one another. In early and late childhood, children need to be increasingly competent in rhythm in order to initiate and sustain one-on-one friendships; as they grow older, errors in rhythm become more costly, especially when children begin socializing in larger groups. If they fail to develop these skills, like Isobel, they may find themselves out of step with their classmates and feeling rejected as a result.

The good news is that school-age children who master these skills have been found to have more positive social attitudes and a higher possibility of forging meaningful friendships later in their lives. This is partly because the ability to pay close attention to another child forms the foundation of other important skills such as listening and empathy, which are essential to fostering deeper connections with others.[6] Rhythm sensitivity also correlates with a child's ability to learn verbal language and reading skills: the more sensitive to rhythm, the greater the reading achievement and use of verbal language too.

RHYTHM IN INFANCY AND EARLY CHILDHOOD

Studies show that children are able to identify and use rhythm very early in their lives. Infants fall asleep more quickly when exposed to rhythm similar to their mothers' heartbeat.[7] When we rock babies to sleep, sing a lullaby, or pat their backs while cooing to them, we are using rhythm not only to connect with them and calm them down, but also to teach them that they are protected and loved.[8] This helps to explain why, when parents enrolled in the federally funded Head Start program were taught to more actively interact with and stimulate their infants and young children by talking, dancing, and singing with them, those children graduated from high school with better self-control and self-esteem than those who did not—and later became more caring and nurturing parents themselves.[9]

TIPS TO HELP INSTILL A SENSE OF RHYTHM IN YOUR VERY YOUNG CHILD

1. Build awareness.

One excellent way to make your very young child more rhythm aware is to simply point out people who are walking, running, driving, or talking in a regular rhythm. Help your child notice when sounds or movements are happening fast or slow: "The dog is running very fast!" "This line is moving very slowly." Over time, she will have a better awareness of how rhythm and tempo are present in so many of our daily activities.

2. Start teaching turn-taking as early as you can.

Whether you were aware of it or not, some of your earliest interactions with your infant were the beginning of teaching her the very important rhythmic skill of turn-taking. When you made silly noises at your baby and she made gurgling noises back at you, this was the beginning of the rhythmic back-and-forth that's so necessary for sharing information and connecting with others.

Throughout early childhood, it's important to reinforce turn-taking, especially as your infant transitions into a toddler. By the age of two, most children are keen to monopolize interactions with others, and they're usually not prepared to wait for a response. During this phase, your own rhythm may be constantly interrupted by your child's urgent demands and needs. You can help your child learn to respect the rhythms of others by teaching her not to interrupt, and to wait her turn before speaking. When your younger child actually waits to take her turn, you can reinforce how much you appreciate this with verbal praise and nonverbal smiles—and every so often with a treat. And you should also model turn-taking with your older children and with your spouse or partner. Time invested in teaching turn-taking during the preschool years will pay off handsomely when your child begins full-time school and has to connect with peers on her own.

3. Sing and dance together.

For generations, parents and grandparents have sung nursery rhymes to babies and little children, bouncing them on their laps and miming along to the words. Although these simple songs have somewhat fallen from fashion, they serve an important purpose: they teach children about rhythm. Jack and Jill, Humpty-Dumpty, and Little Bo-Peep are still great ways to introduce your child to rhythmic patterns of speech. When your child is old enough, you can sing a phrase and then ask her to echo it back to you. Children love to hear such songs repeated over and over and will often demand that you play or sing the same song again and again—they find this kind of repetition reassuring.

Likewise, putting on music and dancing together is a great way to increase her sense of rhythm. Ask her to move to the music and then mirror that movement, taking turns initiating the moves. Resist the temptation to grab your child's hands or arms and move them in time to the beat. While you might think this will help instill a sense of rhythm in your child, she'll learn more if she's allowed to go through the process of figuring out the beat for herself. A music or dance group such as Music Together (see sidebar) is another great way to ensure that your child is exposed to rhythm from an early age.

4. Make a beat and have your child follow it.

As I did with Isobel — the child described at the beginning of the chapter — you can have your child mimic your beat with a drum, rhythm sticks, or even a pair of spoons. Start with a simple, steady rhythm and slowly increase the complexity until your child has difficulty following your lead. Next, you can have your child set the rhythm while you copy it. Then deliberately get the rhythm wrong to see if she notices the difference.

5. Avoid or limit screens.

The American Academy of Pediatrics advises no screen time at all for children until eighteen to twenty-four months, except for video chatting, and that children ages two to five should get an hour or less of screen time per day. We can all model good habits around screen use by putting screens away during mealtimes and other interactions with children. This will give your child greater opportunities to pick up on the rhythms of human-to-human interaction around her and to practice the essential art of syncing up with others.

PLAYING BEAUTIFUL MUSIC TOGETHER

Music Together is a nationwide music education program founded in 1987 by Kenneth Guilmartin that introduces infants and very young children to the language of music.[10] I had heard about Music Together from a number of parents and teachers who touted its effective methods for introducing children to musical basics, but the more I heard about the program, the more I was convinced it could be useful for teaching kids about the rhythmic ebb and flow of human interaction as well. Fortunately, one of my son's best friends is a veteran teacher in the Music Together program, so I asked her if I could attend a class.

The session took place in a brick and steepled Methodist church building one bright, sunny morning. I arrived early so I could observe the moments before class got started. Parents filed in, either holding hands with their young children or carrying their babies in their arms—this was the first class in a series, and everyone was looking a little nervous. Before we all knew it, Miss Gloria, the teacher, began to sing, inviting us to move around to the music. We all laughed a little anxiously, but the rhythm and movement seemed to make us more comfortable.

Soon we were asked to sit in a circle. The children ranged from about eight months to about three plus years. Some children wouldn't sit still for more than a few minutes before jumping up and walking or running around, while others clung to their parents for dear life. Miss Gloria began to play the "Hello" song in a simple beat, saying "hello" to each child in turn— as we all wore name stickers, she could identify everyone by name.

Then it was time for clapping and singing along with a simple and easy-to-remember rhythm. Here, too, some of the children joined in while others wandered around or still mutely clung to a parent. After a few more songs, everyone was handed a willowy piece of cloth and encouraged to stand up and dance while waving the cloth around. Some parents cradled their infants as they moved and waved, others held their children by two hands and swayed in time to the music. Meanwhile, some of the kids were up on their feet copying their parents' dance moves already, while some stayed seated, looking up and bobbing their heads. No child was crying; it was lovely.

As I danced around, I realized that the children weren't the only ones learning; parents were also learning to model rhythm for their children and becoming more acquainted with their child's natural rhythms, in addition to their own. Tom Foote, the creator and program developer of Rhythm Kids—a Music Together program for older children—likes to say that "rhythm is social glue!" and I agree. Through exercises emphasizing turn-taking in music making, repetition, and practice, children aren't only acquiring music skills; they're also learning to listen for and recognize the rhythms around them and adjust their own rhythms in response.

A few months later, I got to return to Miss Gloria's class to see how the parents and children were getting along. I sat and watched while everyone sang, danced, and talked about how things were when they first began and how much they had changed. And, oh my, how they'd changed! Gone was the hesitancy common among the children and their parents during the first class; everyone was so much more comfortable. Even though there still was delightful chaos at times, appropriate turn-taking and sharing were now the norm. But what was most striking to me was the parents. As I sat with them and watched them interact with their children, I thought of a circle of learning going on. Yes, the parents were teaching the children, but at the same time, I couldn't help but notice how the parents were also learning to model what the children needed to see, hear, and do to be part of a social group. Their gestures were bigger, their postures straighter, their voices firmer, their presence more pronounced. Even without the music, there was a wonderful rhythm to their interactions. I wish I could have filmed the group as they mingled before they left because I have a hunch they would have been surprised to see how much they had learned about the music of social interactions.

RHYTHM IN LATE CHILDHOOD

Picture a small child—let's call her Ella—on her first day of kindergarten. She does well in the morning, finding her new classroom easily and cheerfully greeting her new teacher and classmates. But when it comes time for recess, she walks out onto the giant playground and immediately feels overwhelmed and even a little homesick. Children are running around and shouting—but this isn't Ella's thing. She prefers to walk, think, and talk quietly. Determined to make friends, she attempts to join a group playing tag, but though she tries to keep up with the play, she's slow to react to the rapid movements of the other children, and soon the other children stop including her in the game and she is left on the fringes. "They don't like me," Ella concludes, assuming that the other children have rejected her due to her personality, not realizing that she is simply out of step with them.

In late childhood, the point at which children begin to forge meaningful friendships, rhythm is involved at all stages of relationships, especially at the *initiation* phase. If a child is out of sync with the others, she may miss the best moment for initiating a friendship.

However, if a child is struggling to sync up with peers' rhythms in one context—like while running around on the playground—it doesn't necessarily mean that this skill is underdeveloped; it could just mean that the child's natural rhythm doesn't match that of a specific group of kids, or the activity itself. As Ella sadly makes her way toward a bench so she can sit down and rest, she realizes she isn't alone. Beside her is a girl from her class. They look at each other shyly and smile. "Hi, I'm Zoe," the girl says. "Can I sit with you? I don't like to run around." The two girls sit on the bench and suddenly Ella isn't scared or homesick anymore. The two girls sit and chat for the rest of recess.

We've all had the experience of "clicking" with someone on first meeting, but we may not have identified the role that rhythm was playing in that sense of instant connection. Research has shown that synchronicity—or the meshing of our own rhythm with that of another person—can be crucial for providing the comfort needed to get a relationship up and running.[11] In the case of Ella and Zoe, their compatible rhythms immediately brought these two girls into a relationship with each other.

Keep in mind that one rhythm doesn't fit all. Along with learning to modulate her rhythms to match a situation, merely being aware of her natural rhythms will help your child learn to find and initiate a relationship with someone whose rhythm matches hers.

Once children have initiated a friendship and deepened it over time, they will need to learn a different rhythm once they reach the *transition* phase. When the end of the school day or year rolls around, the rhythm most children use to initiate and deepen a connection on the playground may be too energetic for the interactions that should take place when saying goodbye. For Ella and Zoe, that may mean a cautious wave farewell and "see you tomorrow," at the close of the first day of school, and a proper hug and promises to see each other during the summer at the end of the year.

LATE CHILDHOOD IS also the time when children begin to be cognizant of time. I'll never forget the day I was taking my grandson Soren, then six years old, to play basketball at the park, when he turned to me and asked, "What year is this?" I told him it was 2012. "Pappah, is it always 2012?" he asked.

Once children start school, time quickly becomes part of the rhythm that shapes their everyday lives.[12] Although research shows that infants as young as six months of age have some sense of longer and shorter durations of time, their conception of years, hours, and minutes doesn't come into play until about age six, my grandson's age at the time he asked me the question.[13]

In late childhood, an understanding of time becomes extremely important for keeping in sync with the rhythms of everyday life. Like it or not, being on time matters in our society; our ability to do so can affect how others view us and whether or not they wish to engage with us. Although in some Latin American and Asian countries, being late isn't as frowned upon, in the United States, time governs the daily rhythm of our lives. School-age children should be able to understand that when we say to another family, "Let's meet at three to go to the park," we are asking that family to interrupt their rhythm to share with ours, and this means we're expected to show up on time.

In late childhood, kids must learn to read and express time cues accurately or it will create significant social problems for them later on in adolescence, when they're expected to be at class on time and complete assignments on time and will be judged based on their ability to manage their time. Teachers often share with me how frustrating it is when children can't adhere to time cues, such as the bell that signals class is over, or follow time-related instructions such as "one more minute on the assignment and then begin to put away your materials."

Part of the problem is that time is perceived differently by children than it is by adults.[14] In general, time moves much more slowly for children; if you ask a child to sit quietly for ten minutes, those ten minutes can seem like an hour. And research shows that if you ask a child to close her eyes and open them after she thinks a minute has passed, she will open them after about forty seconds. Ask an adult to do the same task and she will keep them closed for seventy seconds. Perhaps now you can appreciate why your child asks, "Are we almost there yet?" on a car ride soon after you pull out of the driveway. Moments like these provide the ideal opportunity to teach your children about time.

TIPS FOR HELPING YOUR CHILD WITH RHYTHM IN LATE CHILDHOOD

1. **Observe how rhythm affects your child in a variety of situations.**

    Since rhythm is learned informally and indirectly, you may not be sure how adept your child is at using this skill. To find out, the first step is to observe your child when interacting with adults and peers. Does your child seem to be out of sync with the other children during a playdate, party, or other activity? Does your child finish the activity earlier or later than everyone else? If your child participates in a music group, do you notice she seems to be out of step with the beat and with others? Does she lag behind or dash ahead when kids are walking in a group or line? Does she persistently interrupt others while speaking? While many of these behaviors are quite normal for a young child, you can help correct them with gentle encouragement and by praising your child when she falls in step with others. If you have other children, you will have the opportunity to observe your child interacting with siblings. Just keep in mind that there's a good chance your children will differ in temperament and rhythm. That's fine as long as they learn to recognize the different rhythms around them and have the ability to adjust their own favored rhythm to match those of others when the situation calls for it.

2. Help your child develop an understanding of time.

One easy way for parents to help children understand this special rhythm that governs our lives is simply by bringing it up in conversation. You can have your child guess how long it will take to drive her from home to some other destination like soccer practice, gymnastics, or birthday parties, or how long it would take to walk to a park. The idea is give your child opportunities to pay attention to the passage of time.

Another way to have your child gain a better understanding of time is by using a time-management chart. You can sit down with your child and work out how much time it takes for her to complete her daily tasks. Perhaps it's ten minutes for getting dressed and five minutes for making the bed. If she is having trouble sticking to her schedule, you can use a timer to see how long it *actually* takes your child to complete these tasks. This will help make time more concrete and understandable for your child. If you wish, you can provide modest rewards for completing tasks on time, but please, nothing major, as these are age-appropriate expectations.

While teachers will be beginning to teach the basics of time in school, it doesn't hurt to have a foundation in the understanding of time beforehand. Even children as young as six can benefit from having a wristwatch and some instruction from parents about time. And make sure to set a good example; if you tell your child you will be up to read with them before bed in five minutes, make sure it is really just five minutes, not seven or ten. And if you tell your child she has ten more minutes to play before leaving for the park, stick to it. It may feel like you are being rigid, but in reality, you are teaching her good habits that will set her up for academic and social development.

3. **Listen to music, dance with your child, or enroll your child in a music or dance group.**

Often, the simplest home-based activities are the most beneficial for young children. Although you can enroll your child in a music or dance class to help improve her sense of rhythm, you can also spend time together listening to music, dancing around the room, or playing instruments together at home. Music Together and Rhythm Kids teachers are trained to encourage children to move their hands, arms, or body along with the beat, to echo a simple pattern by playing percussion or singing, and to create a simple pattern for a grown-up to echo in return. You can use these markers to work with your child at home.

4. **Talk to your child about different tempos and rhythms.**

One of the easiest and most effective ways to improve children's rhythm skills is to increase their awareness of the rhythms all around them and how they differ. You can talk to your child about how some rhythms are fixed and some are movable. The rhythm of the clock ticking can't be changed, but your heart rate can go up and down, you can walk faster or slower, and you can talk at different speeds. Say you're watching a cartoon with your child that features a race car; you can ask your child how the speed is different from that of someone walking. Talk to your child about how certain situations call for different speeds. You can explain to her that running is something we do only outdoors, and that people often speak quickly when they're excited and slow down when they're hesitant or nervous.

5. Remind your child about what he's learned about turn-taking.

Take time to observe your child in different situations to see how he handles turn-taking. For instance, if you're driving a classmate home from school and you overhear the two children talking in the back seat, you can listen to the conversation with your child. Then, after dropping off his friend, you can provide feedback, as in "I liked how you waited for your friend to finish before speaking," or "I heard that your friend hadn't finished speaking before you cut in. Next time try to wait for him to finish speaking first." You can model good turn-taking in your own conversations, too, and even use moments and scenes in movies and on TV to point out when others are doing the same. Mealtimes are another good opportunity to practice turn-taking with your child. You point out the shifts in rhythm and tone of voice signaling that someone is done speaking and ready for a response and show how nods and eye contact will also help him know when it's his turn to speak.

6. **Enroll your child in sports programs or spend time watching sports together.**

Almost all sports require the players to move according to specific rhythms. So, when you enroll your child in a team sport like baseball or soccer, you're helping her learn about how to sync up with others. At home, you can watch a sport on TV with your child and draw her attention to the rhythms going on. For example, during a baseball game batters take their time stretching, swinging, loosening and tightening batting gloves, finding a comfortable stance, and taking a few practice swings before stepping up to the plate and waiting for the pitch. When the pitch is hit, suddenly the batter takes off toward first base and the fielders go into high gear. In this way, you can help her become aware of how these changes in rhythm are an intrinsic part of the game, just as they are a part of life.

WHEN YOUR CHILD NEEDS EXPERT INTERVENTION

If you notice that your child is consistently out of sync with others — and it hasn't gotten better after a month or so of training using the tips described here — it might be time to consult an expert. Checking with your child's teacher is a good place to start. You can ask if he or she has noticed that your child has difficulties with rhythm in the classroom and if the teacher has ideas for how to help. In other instances, your child's teacher may be the first to bring such difficulties to your attention. In either case, if you suspect, as I did with Isobel, that your child is facing real challenges with rhythm, you can have your child assessed by a psychologist who will evaluate her basic psychological abilities, or a learning disability specialist who can assess processing skills. Tests given may include the Biological Rhythm Interview of Assessment in Neuropsychiatry for Kids (BRIAN-K), in which the evaluator will evaluate children's ability to identify and express rhythm.[15]

Professionals involved with teaching music and dance offer a variety of formal tests to assess their pupils' rhythmic abilities, many of which are also often useful in assessing nonverbal rhythmic ability as well.

· · · · · ·

AS YOU HAVE found out, we're immersed in a sea of different rhythms that, though we do not see them, have far-reaching consequences for our relationships. In contrast, facial expressions, the nonverbal channel that follows, are easy to see, but can still have much to do with our ability to connect with others.

CHAPTER 4

Facial Expressions

Smile and the World Smiles with You

I REMEMBER THE DAY LIKE IT WAS YESTERDAY — EVEN THOUGH IT took place nearly forty years ago. I was dead tired. I'd taught a double load of classes, met with my graduate students, and sat through what felt like an endless faculty meeting discussing curricular requirements. After a somewhat harrowing drive on the interstate, I was finally home and looking forward to spending some time with my wife and seven-week-old son, Andy. My wife and I had taken prenatal classes that helped prepare us for what to expect up to and including the birth of our son, but, since then, we really could have used some postnatal classes, which apparently did not exist. The implication was that we would hit some imaginary button and would automatically know how to engage our very young child, but we were still looking for that button. We'd tried to engage Andy countless times with singing, smiles, and silly faces, but for seven weeks we hadn't gotten much of anything back except crying, sleeping, and dirty diapers. We desperately wanted to be good parents and worked hard at it, but the truth was, we were on our own and it was wearing us both down a bit.

Now that I had returned from work, it was my shift. I went into the nursery and found him both awake and in need of a diaper change. I picked him up from the bassinet and put him on the changing table. As I replaced the odorous diaper, chatting with Andy as I always did, I asked him—as though he could answer me—"Whose boy are you? And can you give your daddy a big smile because I worked so hard today?" That's when it happened. Andy began to pump his little arms and legs and *smiled up at me,* for the very first time. Suddenly I was no longer tired. I called my wife, who of course came running in to try her luck, and sure enough within a few minutes Andy gave us another miraculous smile to savor. I've never forgotten that moment. Prior to becoming a parent, I couldn't have imagined the impact a simple facial expression could have on me emotionally. With that exchange of smiles we were connected to each other in a new, exciting way that we hadn't been before.

The smile is perhaps the single most important way in which human beings connect to one another. And it is no accident that an infant's smile carries particular power. Research completed by scientists Morten Kringelbach and his colleagues in the Department of Psychiatry at the University of Oxford found that smiling and overall cuteness appear to affect the brains of caregivers by igniting the brain pleasure systems—the same ones that are triggered by experiences like eating tasty food and listening to good music.[1] Clearly, smiling is one of the gifts evolution has bestowed on infants; it allows them to engage and bond with their caregivers and thus ensure their survival.

As parents, smiles connect us to our children; the first smile of the day at five a.m. brings us joy even if we wish we could go back to sleep; the "hello" smile when we return home lifts our spirits on even the toughest of days. As our children get older, smiles are just as essential to forming and sustaining other relationships, outside the family unit. At the initiating stage of a friendship, a child's smile lets another child know that he welcomes further interaction. In conversation, we use smiles to signal to others that the interaction is going well and that we would like it to continue. At the transition phase, a smile indicates that we enjoyed the time together and hope to repeat it again soon. If I could offer parents only one piece of advice to help their children become socially successful, I would say, "Teach them to smile, and to smile a lot."

Research backs up this advice: smiling may be the single best predictor of children's happiness and social adjustment. Studies show that children who smile more do better with their peers, not only in their ongoing relationships but in initiating new ones as well.[2] And the power of a *genuine* smile continues into adulthood. Psychologists LeeAnne Harker and Dacher Keltner found in a longitudinal study that women whose smiles were rated most "genuine" in college yearbook photos had more fulfilling and longer-lasting marriages and scored higher on tests measuring well-being and happiness *thirty years later*.[3]

Smiles tend to come naturally to children in the early childhood years. According to a study of 1.4 million participants in 166 countries, young children smile more than any other age-group, to the tune of two hundred times a day. That number declines throughout late childhood and into adulthood, dipping to only about twenty smiles a day by age twenty-three, presumably because this is when the worries and responsibilities of adult life take over.[4]

Never have I felt the importance of smiles more profoundly than during my first time back in a classroom after weeks and months of teaching remotely. When I entered the room, there sat sixteen students wearing face masks, everyone silent. Instead of the usual happy hubbub of animated conversations as everyone caught up with one another and exchanged stories of their summers, the atmosphere was almost somber. It felt awful. One of my students summed up the discomfort perfectly: "I miss smiles."

It turns out there are good scientific reasons for why we feel lost and awkward while masked, including the fact that, as developmental psychologist Claus-Christian Carbon points out, masks cover 60 to 70 percent of the face that is relevant for emotional expression.[5] As a scientist, I was interested in finding out exactly how much emotional messaging is lost when wearing masks. Working with colleagues, I decided to experiment with the Diagnostic Analysis of Nonverbal Accuracy

(DANVA) test, which I designed with my colleague Marshall Duke, and which tests the ability to identify emotions using photos of adults and children with different expressions on their faces—only for a portion of this experiment, we covered the lower part of the photographed faces with masks. By contrasting how well people did recognizing emotions on the masked faces versus ones that were not masked, we were able to single out which emotions were more difficult to read when the bottom part of a person's face was covered. Interestingly, fear was the only emotion participants consistently recognized whether faces were masked or not. This is probably because it is an "upper face" emotion expressed primarily by the eyes rather than a "lower face" emotion conveyed by the mouth. Meanwhile, "happy" was most often missed because it is (obviously) communicated largely through a smile. Anger and sadness were also hard to read without the benefit of the lower face, especially when the facial expressions were less pronounced.[6] Considering that happiness, anger, and sadness are arguably the most common emotions we have, the opportunities for misinterpretation are rife.

No wonder masking in classrooms, while necessary for health and safety, caused all kinds of communication problems between teachers and younger students during the pandemic. One third-grade teacher told me about a unique interaction she had with an eight-year-old girl who sheepishly walked up to her desk and asked, "Are you angry at us?" "Angry?" the teacher answered in total surprise. "No, of course I'm not. Whatever gave you that idea?" The young girl explained, "When you put your head to the side, it makes us feel like you're mad at us." Because the teacher's masked facial expressions were more difficult to read, the students were forced to use her posture — a nonverbal channel less often depended on, especially in a classroom situation, and therefore more susceptible to error — to gauge how their teacher was feeling. Unfortunately, the message the little girl had taken away from her teacher's tilted head was inaccurate and could have harmed the student-teacher relationship. While masking, and the social isolation of the pandemic more generally, robbed all children of opportunities to experience the types of social interaction through which the meanings of facial expressions, especially subtle ones, are learned, children making the transition from early to late childhood probably suffered the most. As these children move into late childhood and adolescence, parents and teachers may need to help them make up this lost ground by more directly teaching the skills involved both in reading and in expressing emotions through this nonverbal channel.

But the pandemic isn't the only reason why many children are falling behind in their ability to read and convey emotion through facial expression. As every parent knows, today's children were spending less time with one another in person and more time fixated on screens even before the pandemic — a problem exacerbated by the fact that many adults around them are on screens to a similar degree, thereby offering fewer opportunities for parents to model appropriate facial expressions, as faces tend to be fairly blank when staring at a phone or laptop.

And when children communicate with their peers and with the adults in their life via text, of course, facial expressions are absent altogether.

Although emoticons and emojis are intended to make the emotional meaning of messages in emails and texts clearer, it is important to keep in mind that though many emoticons and emojis resemble faces, they are not processed within the brain in the same way as actual faces. When you see an expression of emotion in real life, areas of the brain that process emotions get triggered. But when you see an emoji or emoticon on your phone, your brain processes it more like a graph—you absorb the information intellectually rather than emotionally. Although an emoji might look like a nonverbal communication, it isn't.[7] You can't tell whether the message is sincere or insincere, sarcastic or earnest. Rather than clarifying our verbal meanings, emojis and emoticons mostly emphasize what already is obvious in the words we use. My recommendation for children in late childhood, therefore, is to use emoticons and emojis sparingly when communicating with them and for adults to check in with children to make sure they are clear on the emotional meanings of those symbols sent to them and those they send to others in return.

Zoom and other types of video meetings pose further problems for children's nonverbal development. After all, facial expressions on Zoom do not mirror those we use in person. In typical Zoom interactions we are largely immobile, staring for minutes at a time, and are stared back at for minutes at a time. This is the antithesis of what typically happens when two people interact with one another face-to-face. On Zoom, it's considered rude to look away when someone is speaking, but in person, it's actually perfectly acceptable to glance away from someone while talking to them. In fact, if someone stares at you too long during an in-person interaction, it can be unsettling. In person, we move and shift around, offering different perspectives on our facial expressions to our partners, and may come closer or move farther away from each other, depending on how the interaction is going. The need to maintain prolonged eye contact with a person's disembodied face extremely close to us simply doesn't exist outside of Zoom. Children who spend hours learning on Zoom, therefore, are missing out on time spent practicing appropriate eye contact in person.

Fortunately, research has shown that when teachers were given training in the use of facial expressions (and gestures) for their Zoom classes, their students were more likely to retain academic information and test higher than students of teachers who did not receive the training. Not only did the students learn more, but it turned out they liked those teachers better than those who hadn't taken the training.[8]

While smiles and eye contact are critically important, they are not the only facial expressions available to us. As I'll show in this chapter, we have an entire palette of expressions at our disposal. Like painters, we need to use all these different hues to convey our emotions and be successful in our interactions with others. And while most infants and young children will smile—as well as grimace, frown, and pout—instinctively, without having to be taught, the ability to use or read other facial expressions doesn't come as naturally. This chapter will show how you can help your child learn how to better express himself via his facial features and, in turn, how to better interpret the expressions of others.

WHY FACIAL EXPRESSIONS MATTER

Despite having studied nonverbal communication for decades, it was only a few years ago that I truly realized just how much we rely on facial expressions to forge connections with others. I had been asked to give a talk on nonverbal communication to a group of people diagnosed with a somewhat rare and potentially debilitating congenital disorder called Moebius syndrome. This condition is characterized by (along with other symptoms) an inability to change facial expressions because of a lack of innervation of facial muscles. As I stood up to begin my presentation, I looked out at the unchanging, emotionally blank expressions of the people in the audience in front of me, unable to tell if they were engaged, pleased, bored, angry, or dissatisfied with me, a stranger coming to talk to them about a topic they understood more intimately than I ever could. I realized then, in a way I haven't forgotten since, how difficult relationships must be for this group of people — and how courageous they were to continue to pursue them.

Facial expressions are crucial to relationships because they serve a very important function: the sending and receiving of emotional information. For most people, our emotions are literally written all over our faces. When we communicate with one another in person we're constantly sending out signals using our facial expressions, whether we are speaking or silent. We have an incredible forty-three different muscles in our faces, allowing us to produce more than ten thousand discriminable expressions that communicate a remarkable range of emotions. Even a simple smile can be a complex matter, requiring the use of our eyes, mouth, and other facial movements. As it turns out, there are at least nineteen different types of smiles—each with a different meaning—and surprisingly, only six communicate that someone is having a good time![9]

In order to be fully expressive, we can wrinkle our noses, furrow our foreheads, lift our eyebrows, purse our lips, and use our eyes to communicate what we're feeling. When we're face-to-face with another person, we're constantly scanning his or her face for clues and information. Is that person feeling bored or tired? Curious or doubtful? Concentrating or confused? Disgusted or angry? Excited or tense? For someone who is not skilled at reading facial expressions, disgust can look a lot like anger, curiosity is easy to misread as skepticism, and so on. Expressions can vary in intensity too, from a rapid smirk to a wide, long-lasting grin—to name only two of the myriad ways we can use our faces to express ourselves.

What's curious is that despite the complexity of facial expressions, most children are not taught their meaning in school. Instead, they are left to figure out this important communication mode for themselves, sometimes making more than a few mistakes along the way.

Unlike the often-unrecognized aspects of rhythm that operate outside of our conscious attention, facial expressions are difficult to ignore; they are right there on our faces for everyone to see and react to. But while *others* can see our expressions, we can't see our own, and as a result, most of us are quite unaware of what our face looks like when we are feeling anger, happiness, surprise, and so on — and even when we are not feeling a strong emotion at all. Understanding the signals they are sending with their own facial language is a complex skill that children (and adults) can only acquire over time and with practice.

On the whole, psychologists agree that facial expressions are much more powerful than the words we use.[10] For example, when someone tells you he's having a great time with a depressed look on his face, you will be much more inclined to believe his facial expression than his verbal statement. To complicate the matter, however, facial expressions may be the easiest of all the nonverbal channels to fake. Children as young as four years of age are able to produce a convincingly happy expression to cover up their true feelings.[11] In fact, adults sometimes *actively teach* children to cover up their feelings in this way, asking them to smile and say thank you for an unwanted gift rather than frowning and pouting, for example. Many of the aspects of our early training in what might be included under the heading of "manners" or "social graces" are in fact teaching children to conceal their emotions via their facial expressions, and they only become better at this with age. But while there are times when we might be able to successfully cover up our true feelings, we can't hide the fact that our faces are out there for everyone to see.[12]

Perhaps it's because facial expressions are so visible that scientists have published more studies on them than on all the other nonverbal channels combined, with more than fifteen thousand articles written in the past ten years (based on a PubMed search). These modern-day studies of facial expressions can be traced back to the nineteenth-century French physician Guillaume-Benjamin-Amand Duchenne, who stimulated the faces of patients with electricity to see which muscles were involved in making a particular expression. His work gave rise to the phrase "Duchenne smile," referring to a genuine smile that goes all the way up to the eyes. The photographs Duchenne took of his patients also helped to inspire Charles Darwin's study *The Expression of Emotions in Man and Animals*, in which Darwin suggested that seven basic emotions were expressed similarly across all cultures of the world: happy, sad, angry, fearful, disgusted, surprised, and contemptuous.[13]

Since then, there's been some debate around whether these expressions are recognized universally, and it seems that our cultural backgrounds do play a large part in the ways in which we're able to recognize emotions in others, especially if those expressions are less intense. Studies by psychologist Paul Ekman in the 1960s provided support for Darwin's suggestion of universally recognized emotions in faces, but later research seems to suggest that while more pronounced facial expressions are familiar across cultures, many of the subtler expressions we use in everyday interactions are determined and modified according to where we come from.[14]

Cross-cultural psychologist David Matsumoto and his colleagues, for example, found that Americans rate the same expressions of happiness, sadness, and surprise more intensely than most Japanese people, who also express these emotions less intensely. Matsumoto suggests that this occurs because Japanese people are taught to be less emotive from a very early age.[15] Another study found that Chinese people rely on the eyes more when communicating via facial expressions, while here in America and Europe, we're more likely to rely on the eyebrows and mouth.[16]

If you are white, it's especially important to be aware of unconscious racial bias that may be affecting your ability to accurately read facial expressions. In fact, research has found that white Americans are less adept at reading emotions in the facial expressions of Black Americans compared to those of other white people. Moreover, when white Americans misinterpreted emotions in Black American faces, they were most likely to identify anger when it wasn't there—which obviously has major implications for how Black children are treated in interactions with white peers (as well as with teachers, public safety officers, and other adults).[17] In a recent study by developmental psychologist Amy Halberstadt and her colleagues, when 178 predominantly white, prospective teachers were asked to identify emotion in seventy-two different children's photos, they identified the Black children as having angry facial expressions even when they were showing other emotions. This is why teacher workshops and education focused on raising awareness of racial bias in nonverbal communication should be required as they are for racial bias in verbal communication, and why parents should also play a role in making their children aware of bias from a young age.[18]

Overall, we're typically much better at reading emotions in facial expressions of people we know the best, beginning with our own family members, and often extending to members of our own cultural and racial group as well. So, it's important to always be aware of the possibility of making errors, and to reinforce this awareness in your child by explaining that different people have different ways of communicating and that, when initiating new relationships, it's a good idea to slow down and take the time to make sure that we are reading someone's emotions correctly.

FACIAL EXPRESSIONS IN INFANCY AND EARLY CHILDHOOD

I was overjoyed to see my baby son beaming up at me when he was still only seven weeks old. He, like other babies, came into the world with poor eyesight and little ability to control his facial features or react to those of his caregivers. With time, however, babies' brains develop in response to the people in their environment, and by two months or so they begin to recognize you and respond accordingly. Eventually they will smile on their own and invite you to smile in return. This is social interaction in its most basic form. There is some disagreement among psychologists as to whether identifying emotion in others' facial expressions precedes or follows the ability to express emotions of their own, but both begin to appear with some regularity within the first four to six weeks.

Although some basic facial expressions are hardwired from birth, interactions between caregivers and children are the main way very young children learn to pick up emotions via facial cues. At first, you'll tend to instinctively use big, exaggerated facial expressions with your child, but these will naturally become more subtle as he grows older and becomes more adept at reading the basic emotions of happiness, sadness, anger, and fear in the faces of caregivers. Even before your child can use words or understand concepts, he can sense a great deal simply by looking at your face—this is how infants know whether they are safe or not. One study even showed that babies could be encouraged to crawl across a gap that looked like a precipitous drop—but that was actually covered with a piece of plexiglass—as long as a mother stood at the other side encouraging the child with the nonverbal cues of facial expressions and tones of voice.[19]

Toward the end of your child's first year, he will begin to look at the faces of others for hints about how to regulate his own emotional behavior. This is called "social referencing." For example, if you have a worried look on your face, chances are your child will become worried as well. Somewhere between the ages of nine and eighteen months, caregivers and infants become involved in "joint attention," which Amy Halberstadt, a professor at North Carolina State University who has studied nonverbal communication for decades, has identified as one of the most significant nonverbal developmental markers.[20]

This is when a child and caregiver look at each other and then an object—for example, a dog—and then the caregiver glances at the dog and then back at the child smiling while saying "There's a doggie"; then they both return their gaze to the dog, and the caregiver continues to repeat the word "doggie." This seemingly simple interaction has major implications not only for learning nonverbal cues but for learning verbal language as well. Your smile makes the child feel safe, the word "doggie" becomes associated with the dog walking toward him, and, with repetition, the word becomes part of the child's vocabulary. (As an added benefit, your child may also associate happy feelings with the presence of dogs.)

It's also a uniquely human interaction.[21] Scientists who have taken on the task of raising a primate along with a human child note that nonhuman primates can do many of the developmental tasks better than the human infants, but when it comes to being able to perform "joint attention," they fail to match their human peers.[22]

Beginning at around six months and lasting through about eighteen months, your child will often add the nonverbal channel of touch into the mix and explore others' faces with his hands. There are few experiences more delightful than having a small child push the edges of your mouth upward to create a smile and hearing him laugh with delight when he's done.

FACIAL EXPRESSIONS

Throughout this period in your child's development, you should keep in mind that very young children are much better at communicating via facial expressions than they are at reading them, as a study conducted by developmental psychologist Tiffany Field showed.[23] Interestingly, at this age negative emotions are more difficult for children to communicate and read than positive ones. Although your child may sense when something is wrong, he may not yet be able to discriminate between expressions of sadness, anger, and fear. Since an inability to correctly communicate negative emotions can lead to misunderstandings even for very young children, it's important to keep this discrepancy in mind and actively point out the various facial expressions and their significance.

Taking care of a young child can be an emotional business, causing you to experience a range of feelings over the course of the day; sometimes, your emotions will swing wildly from minute to minute. Because infants, toddlers, and even preschool-age children don't yet have the ability to tend to their own needs, they are constantly demanding something from the adults around them. It is impossible not to get frustrated, irritated, or upset at times with such unrelenting interruptions, but rather than try to ignore those feelings, you can use them as teachable moments: opportunities to model what these negative emotions look like, as well as how to deal with them. When you are irritated, tell the child, "I'm feeling irritated right now. I bet you can see it in my face. I'm going to go across the room and sit for a minute until I feel better. When I'm done, I'll come back, and I'll have a much happier face for you."

TIPS TO HELP YOUR VERY YOUNG CHILD WITH FACIAL EXPRESSIONS

1. **Practice making a range of facial expressions on your own.**

   The primary way infants and children in early childhood learn to express themselves via this channel (and others) is by mimicking their caregivers. As most adults don't spend a lot of time analyzing their own facial expressions, it's worth taking some time to look in the bathroom mirror in order to evaluate your own ability to express happiness, sadness, anger, and fear. Then try out your newfound expressiveness with your child. As a side benefit, the bigger and more exaggerated you can make your facial expressions with very young children, the more they will connect and engage with you.

2. **Practice making a range of facial expressions with your child.**

   Like all the nonverbal channels, facial expressions are rarely taught directly—but they can be. When your child is a baby, you can play simple games such as peekaboo and "Who is that in the mirror?" to help him gain practice in reading faces and an understanding of the way his own face communicates emotion in return. As your child grows and acquires language, you can continue to make faces with him and encourage him to make faces with differing degrees of intensity (for example, a "mad" face, then a "really mad" face, then a face that's only "a little bit mad") back at you.

FACIAL EXPRESSIONS

You can also teach your child some general rules about the context in which these expressions are appropriate and inappropriate. For example, "You just got the big ice cream cone you wanted, and you are really happy. Make a happy face!" Then: "Oh my! You just dropped your ice cream cone, it's spoiled, and you are really sad. Make a sad face." In this way, your child will begin to connect facial expressions with feelings and with the scenarios in which he can use these nonverbal cues to express himself.

3. Use photos.

You can look through photos on your phone with your child, asking her to spot and name different expressions, then connect them to the relevant emotion, such as "Grandma is smiling, so she is happy"; "my brother is scowling, so he is upset." Young children tend to enjoy posing for and taking photos, so you can even play a game of "model and photographer," taking turns with the camera while the other person smiles, grimaces, and makes a surprised or fearful face. Then you can look at the photos together and talk about the different emotions and how successful you were at conveying them.

4. Read picture books and talk about the emotions you can see in the characters' faces.

Many children's books feature characters that go on emotional journeys over the course of the narrative. As you read to your child, anytime there is an emotion displayed in an illustration, you can point to it and ask him to name it. The

Elephant and Piggie books, written and illustrated by Mo Willems, are particularly well suited to this. After you've finished the story, you can talk to your child about how Gerald the elephant expresses himself using his face as well as his words, and how his best friend, Piggie, responds. Then you and your child can play around mimicking the faces of the characters in the book.

Singing old-fashioned nursery rhymes can also be a good prompt. When you get to the end of the rhyme, ask your child to (nonverbally) express the emotion consistent with the ending. How does he feel about Jack falling down and Jill coming tumbling after? Can he make a facial expression to show that emotion?

5. Be mindful of your own facial expressions when you're around your young child.

Most parents and caregivers aren't aware of how much emotional information their children—particularly very young children—pick up in their facial expressions. If you're upset by something that doesn't have anything to do with your child—and your face shows anger, sadness, or fear as a result—your child may react as though those emotions were meant for him. (We sometimes make that same mistake as adults when our partners or spouses are upset about something that has nothing to do with us—but unlike very young children, we can use verbal language to investigate whether the emotions are directed at us or not.) Keep this in mind when you're with your

FACIAL EXPRESSIONS

child and make sure your expressions are consistent with any messages you'd wish him to receive.

6. Make sure to sit down for mealtimes with your child.

One simple but powerful way to give your child additional opportunities to observe and practice facial expressions is to prioritize family meals—and make the dining table a screen-free zone. Research shows that one of the best sources of nonverbal learning is time spent eating together as a family. Moreover, children whose families eat together more than three times a week have better relationships, do better at school, are more resilient in the face of adversity, and are less likely to get into trouble.[24]

During mealtimes, you can model appropriate facial expressions—and appropriate interactions in general—for your child. When you include others, such as extended family and friends, not only do you give your child exposure to a greater range of all types of nonverbal behaviors and styles, but you also show him how relationships work and how important they are. I can still remember my grandfather telling me the story over dinner of how when he first saw my grandmother's warm smile it so captivated him, even from a distance, that he just had to meet and learn more about her—that smile became the reason for my existence! Family mealtimes offer children a wealth of nonverbal learning opportunities and are well worth taking the time to build into your day.

FACIAL EXPRESSIONS IN LATE CHILDHOOD

I first met Michael, a third grader, when I visited his school at the request of his school counselor, who told me she found him to be a delightful child and wondered why he was having so much difficulty making friends. On a school visit, I observed Michael sitting at a lunch table alone and was struck immediately by his facial expression. His mouth was tightly pursed, and his nose was scrunched up as if he were smelling or tasting something awful. Later I approached Michael at the lunch table and asked him how he was feeling. He replied that he wasn't feeling anything in particular, even though his resting facial expression told a very different story. As we talked, I realized Michael was completely unaware of how his resting face looked and how off-putting it was to his peers.

In late childhood, all that children have learned about facial expressions is put to the test when they begin full-time school. Before then, parents often function as a coach, pointing out their child's errors in reading and expressing emotions in faces. ("You shouldn't be smiling, Cassie, you hurt Taylor's feelings! See, you've made him cry.") But when full-time schooling begins, parents must share these coaching duties: first with teachers and then with their children's peers, who will provide difficult but potentially useful feedback about their nonverbal behavior.

In fact, facial expressions play a significant role in the success or failure of all four phases of relationships (choice, initiating, deepening, and transition phases). Our *resting face,* the facial expression our face has when we are not feeling any specific emotion, is especially crucial when we are choosing and initiating relationships effectively. When we are looking around the room at a party or event to decide whom we would like to initiate a conversation with, we are more likely to choose someone whose facial expression is positive and inviting rather than someone who looks sad, afraid, or angry. The same is true for children.

An awareness of what our resting face is communicating to others is key for getting relationships off to a good start. Most of us—including adults—have no idea what our face looks like when it is resting, but luckily, this is quite easy to learn. In Michael's case, after he was made aware, and after we tried out some different expressions in the mirror, he was able to adjust his resting face to more accurately convey how he was actually feeling. And from his counselor's subsequent report, it was clear that he was soon getting on much better with his schoolmates.

EYE CONTACT, A SPECIAL KIND OF FACIAL EXPRESSION

Eye contact is a powerful form of communication with very strict rules governing how and how long we gaze at one another. If you've ever had a conversation with someone who stares directly at you without breaking eye contact for the length of the interaction, you know how uncomfortable this can make you feel. On the other hand, if someone avoids eye contact with you altogether, it can make them appear furtive or nervous. So, a balance is required.

Eye contact is a tricky thing to teach because it's so intuitive and context dependent. How much is too much eye contact and how much is too little? When do we look at each other's faces and when do we look away? How do we show we're interested in what is being said without making others uncomfortable by overdoing our attention? Here's how to explain eye contact rules in simple terms for your child: "You should spend more time looking at others when you're listening than you do when you're speaking."

In the previous chapter, I suggested that rhythm and timing were often intertwined with the other nonverbal communication channels, and eye contact is one of them. If we want our children's relationships to get off to a good start and have a chance to deepen later, we must encourage them to learn the appropriate timing for making and breaking eye contact.

In fact, how long one maintains eye contact is as important as how often. Two to four seconds is considered acceptable. Less than that is "darting" and longer than that is "staring." In general, children (and adults) should follow the 50/70 rule. That is, make eye contact for about 50 percent of the time while speaking and roughly 70 percent of the time while listening.[25]

Modeling good eye contact for your child can start from day one. With infants, you can make sure to look them in the eye when feeding, putting them to bed, and playing. When a toddler asks for food or a toy, you can wait for him to make eye contact before you respond, and when teaching him to say "please" and "thank you," you can show him that these phrases should be accompanied by eye contact. Taking time away from screens to be present for your child will give you more opportunities to model good eye contact as well.

While a year-plus of Zoom school has, as noted earlier in the chapter, interfered with many children's ability to use eye contact correctly in social interactions, older children can be taught these skills directly. If your school-age child looks away while saying something to you, you can say, "You are speaking to the wall, and I am over here." You can also positively reinforce eye contact by using phrases like, "I love it when you look at me when I talk to you" and "Thank you for looking at me; now I can see your big brown eyes, and it helps me to know how you feel."

At the same time, you can teach your child about the difference between staring and glancing; you can even have a staring contest with your child to prove your point. Then explain that the correct amount of time to look at someone is two to four seconds, and practice gauging longer and shorter time periods with her.

Keep in mind that, like other facial expressions, eye contact can be culturally determined. In the United States, children are taught to smile and make eye contact to initiate a relationship. However, in some Asian and Middle Eastern countries, direct eye contact is considered rude or even aggressive. In Chinese culture, children are often instructed to keep their eyes lowered when interacting with one another and especially when interacting with adults, as eye contact is a sign of disrespect. Teachers and parents need to be aware of these differences and help children become aware as well.[26]

TIPS FOR HELPING YOUR CHILD WITH FACIAL EXPRESSIONS IN LATE CHILDHOOD

1. Observe what your child's face is saying.

Next time you have the opportunity, observe your child within a group of children of a similar age. Watch as they eat, play, and speak to one another in order to see how well your child uses facial expressions to express his emotions. Does he make eye contact with others or spend a lot of time looking away or to the ground? Does he notice other children's facial expressions, perhaps going over to play with a child who is looking sad? Does he smile with excitement when someone includes him in a game? It's also important to find out what your child's resting face is communicating. Watch for those situations in which your child is looking out a window or sitting quietly with a book and observe what the resting face looks like or scroll through photos of your child to see if he has a characteristic expression when he is not looking at the camera or posing. Then note what this expression appears to be communicating emotionally.

2. Use stories.

One way to teach your child about facial expressions is through stories. If your child is telling you about something that happened at school, you could ask him, "How did so-and-so feel about that?" and "How could you tell?" Explain that different situations require different expressions. You can say,

"A big happy smile when you see a friend is a great way to greet them," or "If your friend is feeling sad, you can make a sad face to let them know you understand." When you're looking at books or magazines with your child, ask him what each expression is showing. Another idea is to watch TV programs or movies with your child and then turn the sound off so he can concentrate on the facial expressions. Hit pause at various places and ask your child how he thinks the character feels in that moment, and why. Daytime soaps are an especially good source of facial expressions of emotions at all levels of intensity—just make sure the content is age-appropriate!

3. Talk to your child about his resting face.

First, introduce the concept of a resting face to your child, and explain how important it is to have a happy, welcoming resting face so that others will want to come over and play with him. You can show your child photos of his own resting face or ask him to identify the resting faces of others when you're out walking or on public transport. Then have your child practice different versions of his resting face in the mirror and talk about what they communicate.

4. Enroll your child in theater or improv classes.

Getting involved in any kind of drama or theater program is a great way for children to hone their skill in facial expressions, as of course these are one of the primary ways that actors express what characters are feeling. When your child is learning how to communicate his character's emotion to the audience, he's learning how to express himself when off the stage as well.

WHEN YOUR CHILD NEEDS EXPERT INTERVENTION

If you feel your child is really struggling with facial expressions, you can have an expert administer the Diagnostic Analysis of Nonverbal Accuracy (DANVA). Experts can use these results to identify which emotions children can and cannot identify (at both high and low intensity).

* * * * * *

MOST OF US are acutely aware of the important role facial expressions play in our interactions with one another, but we tend to pay less attention to the physical space through which these emotional messages must travel. Yet, the ability to adhere to the accepted rules governing personal space has significance for how our relationships turn out, as you will learn in the chapter that follows.

CHAPTER 5

Personal Space

That's Close Enough

Every Tuesday for the past twenty-seven years, I've left the confines of the Emory campus and driven out into the greater Atlanta community to consult with the staff of a program responsible for treating severely emotionally disturbed children and adolescents. Because of the nature of the diagnoses, I'm never quite sure what to expect when I arrive at the center. On one spring morning, I walked through the doors of the main entrance and began my circuit around the building to check in with staff about problems they were encountering with the children. As I walked into one of the classrooms, a gangly six-foot-tall fourteen-year-old named Raul, who was sitting in the front row, got up from his desk and began walking toward me.

I watched his approach with interest and waited for him to stop and say something, but he just kept coming forward. I decided to stay put and see how close he would come before he stopped. When he did come to a halt we were just about nose to nose. Inches from my face, he said, "Good morning, Dr. Nowicki. How are you?" I could feel his breath on me, and it was difficult to bring his face into focus.

"I'm fine, Raul. How are you?" I replied.

"I'm fine too," he answered. "It's a nice day, isn't it?"

"Yes, it is, but it would be an even nicer day if you took just one step back." Then I asked him to put his arm out in front of him to measure the space between us and said, "That's about the right distance you should be away from others when you greet them."

Unbeknownst to me, the staff had been working with Raul on improving social skills—especially how he greeted others—and had decided to test what they had taught Raul on me. But while the staff had successfully given Raul the appropriate words to use when greeting someone in the morning, they had apparently forgotten to teach him about the equally important nonverbal communication channel of personal space: the invisible bubble between ourselves and others through which most of our nonverbal messages must pass.

WHY PERSONAL SPACE MATTERS

Like other animals, we humans evolved with a natural instinct to protect our territory from outside interlopers. We notice if a stranger appears in our front yard. We become concerned if an unknown car enters our driveway (even if it is just to back out and go in another direction). When we have dinner guests or throw parties, we would not be thrilled to find a guest rummaging through the drawers in our bedroom. And we are equally possessive about our personal space, the portable force field that extends out from our bodies and into our social world.

When someone encroaches on our personal space, as Raul did with me, it usually triggers what's known as a "flight" reaction, a reflexive response to threat. We shrink back or step sideways; we try to reclaim the space we've lost. Personal space researcher and neuropsychologist Michael Graziano has identified the specialized neurons in the brain that activate this instinctive response. He calls them peripersonal neurons and explains that they act like Geiger counters, scanning our immediate surrounding area, gathering relevant information about how far away other people or objects are, then triggering a response when they sense our personal space is being encroached upon.[1] Want to see this monitoring system in action? Just watch how crowds of people crossing a street from opposite corners avoid crashing into one another—even though some walkers are not paying attention to one another or are even looking down at their phones. It really is quite astonishing.

To help my psychology students at Emory better understand the function of their peripersonal neurons and become more aware of their personal space boundaries, I usually stage a classroom demonstration. I ask two students to stand at opposite sides of the room—about twenty or so feet apart—and then tell them to start walking toward each other. Then I ask them to stop as soon as they begin to feel uncomfortable. They will usually slow to a complete halt at about a four-foot distance from the other person (though this will invariably vary depending on their gender and cultural background). What doesn't vary, however, is what the students do when they reach their threshold of comfort: they not only choose to stop but they rock backward as though they have bumped into something solid. Their peripersonal neuronal warning system has been activated, warning them of threat.

As we go about our everyday lives, we're always trying to maintain a comfortable distance from others. Whether we're aware of it or not, we are constantly adjusting this calculation depending on where we are, whom we're with, and how we feel. When we feel anxious, we step away from others to protect ourselves. When we feel comfortable and at ease, we allow others to come closer.

In his 1966 book, *The Hidden Dimension,* cultural anthropologist Edward T. Hall described what are still considered the accepted zones of personal space for most Americans.[2] The first of these is the *intimate zone,* and it extends out to about eighteen inches. We usually permit only close friends and family into this space. When operating within this space, we tend to exchange private information and feelings, lowering our voices if there are others in the room so that only those in our intimate space can hear the exchange. (For children, learning to control the volume of their voices within this closest zone is sometimes difficult, and they may whisper loudly.)

Just beyond the intimate zone is the *personal region,* extending out to about four feet or so. A significant number of our everyday interactions take place within this zone. When you meet an acquaintance on the street, this is the usual amount of space you will leave between the two of you; the same distance you might leave when speaking to a clerk in a store or a neighbor at the end of the driveway. While speech is louder here than in the intimate zone, it still is relatively private. If someone happens to walk past such an interaction between two people, they may overhear what is being said, but norms dictate they will make every attempt to ignore it and not join in.

The next zone is what Hall calls our *social space,* which stretches from four feet out to around twelve feet. We can raise our voices in this zone because we intend for others to be able to hear what we are discussing. A tour guide or a teacher standing in a classroom of twenty students might make use of this zone. Because we are easily seen and heard in this space, intimate or personal matters tend not to be discussed here.

Finally, we have the *public zone,* which extends out beyond the twelve-foot limit of the social zone. Public events such as speeches occur in this space, but not much social interaction. At this distance, we can read what someone's posture might be telling us, but our gestures and other nonverbal behaviors have to be more exaggerated to be noticed.

Regardless of distance, our peripersonal neurons constantly monitor each one of these zones for signs of threat. Hall notes that we share with animals an innate ability to quickly establish our level of comfort with intruders, but unlike animals, we learn to modify these calculations based on experiences with our families, our communities, and the prevailing social norms. As a result, the size of our space bubbles will, to a certain degree, depend on the behaviors we observed in our home, as well as the country and culture into which we are born. For example, people from the United States and the United Kingdom have the biggest space bubbles, whereas people from Southern Europe and the Middle East are happy to be in much closer range.[3]

Sometimes, however, we are forced to adapt to a situation in which our bubble is invaded by a complete stranger. Picture yourself standing alone in the back of an empty elevator. Your posture is relaxed, slightly slumped. The elevator stops at a floor, the doors open, and the scene changes dramatically as someone enters. You immediately stand up straighter, and then you and the new passenger mentally divide up the elevator territory into equal halves and you each instinctively retreat to your side. However, as more passengers enter, the elevator becomes crowded, forcing your personal space bubble to contract, allowing complete strangers into a zone where you would usually feel threatened. How are we able to continue standing in the elevator without our peripersonal neurons telling us to flee? By doing everything we can to convince ourselves that we're actually alone. We look straight ahead, eyes glued to the doors, or we stare downward at the floor or at our phone. (We do a version of this for hours on end when sitting next to a stranger on an airplane, as well.) Next time you find yourself in an elevator with multiple people, turn your head slightly (about five degrees) to the right or left and see what happens. This slight head movement destroys the illusion of being alone—for all of you—and you are likely to get a somewhat hostile nonverbal reaction from the person next to you, a sort of "What are you looking at?" expression.

While Hall envisioned these zones as a series of concentric rings with us at the center, research I conducted with Marshall Duke, my colleague at Emory, suggests that our personal space bubbles aren't shaped like perfect circles. In our study, we took a simple drawing of a room with a dot in the center and concentric circles going out to the periphery. We asked thousands of individuals to imagine themselves standing in the center of the room. Then we asked them to indicate where they would like various people of different ages, genders, and races to stop when walking toward them from the front, back and sides (for younger children we used Fisher-Price figures to make the visualization task easier for them). The study provided us with a wealth of information about learned norms around personal space, including a detailed picture of what our personal space zones look like.[4]

The first thing we noticed is that people's personal space bubbles were deeper at the back than at the front. This makes sense as the primary function of personal space is to act as an early warning system to protect us from physical harm. People can both see and hear possible threats approaching from the front but can only use sound when evaluating threats coming from behind. As a result, they need extra space behind them in order to feel safe. From these data, we constructed the

Comfortable Interpersonal Distance (CID) scale, which measures the preferred interpersonal distance as a function of race, age, and gender. In general, we found that women seem to prefer more space around them than men, and older adults seem to require more distance than younger ones. Young children have the smallest protective space bubble of all—but they're a lot less discerning about whom they let into their personal space zone than adults.[5]

Not only does allowing for the correct amount of personal space help make others feel more comfortable around us; it provides the medium through which other nonverbal behaviors such as facial expressions, postures, gestures, vocalics, and touch must pass. The greater the distance, the harder it is to pick up on emotional cues from the other nonverbal channels; faces become more difficult to read and tones of voice become more challenging to identify. Equally, if someone is standing too close, we feel encroached upon and have a harder time focusing on that person's facial expressions or gestures. So, children who have difficulty understanding personal space can struggle in manifold ways.

Neuropsychologist Michael Graziano had spent his career studying personal space, but nothing could have prepared him for what happened when his four-year-old son started having problems at school. Graziano's son was happy, smart, and talkative, but the young boy had difficulties moving through space and would frequently trip, crash into furniture, and fall out of his chair. The problems escalated when he began first grade, when teachers perceived his rocking and jiggling at his desk as sexual gestures and his accidental bumping into others as a form of sexual assault. The boy's school even reported Graziano and his wife to child protective services as possible child abusers. Eventually, experts were able to present a different and science-based interpretation of the boy's behavior. It turned out that Graziano's son was suffering from dyspraxia. Those with this disorder experience a variety of difficulties, but in the boy's case the most striking symptom was the malfunctioning of his peripersonal neurons. This intervention cleared the parents' names, and the child was able to receive the help he needed, albeit at another school.[6]

As one of the leading researchers in the discovery of neural mechanisms underlying the use of personal space, Graziano understood why his son could not correctly process where his body was in relation to others. But he was still stunned by the real-life consequences of his son's inability to finesse his movements in the space around him. "I studied personal space in the lab. For years I studied the brain basis of it," he wrote in his book, *The Spaces between Us*. "But I was in no way prepared for its full human dimensions.... Personal space is the fundamental scaffold of human interaction... a vast invisible presence affecting us all of the time."[7] It was this experience with his son that opened Graziano's eyes to how truly important managing personal space can be, even for someone as young as four years old.

Ask any teacher and they will tell you about their experiences with "space invaders" in the classroom: children who constantly hover, touch, and violate the personal space of others. Although these behaviors are usually not the result of a severe neurological disorder—as was the case with Graziano's son—even trivial mistakes can have very real personal consequences. If a child repeatedly invades the space of other children—even when this happens accidentally and without malice—you can bet that the child's classmates will learn to keep a wide berth, leading to feelings of social isolation for the child if not corrected.

During the pandemic, of course, children were explicitly taught about personal space in the form of social distancing. Outlines of feet were painted on floors and colorful tape appeared on sidewalks and hallways reminding them how far away they were supposed to stand from others. The six-foot rule, which was so helpful in the public health crisis, also had the unfortunate side effect of obliterating the traditional interpersonal zones we have long used. Harvard Medical School professor Daphne Holt found that during the pandemic, personal space preferences had increased 40 to 50 percent on average in people she tested, especially if they perceived a higher overall risk of being infected with COVID-19. Interestingly, however, those who were more frightened about catching the virus kept greater distances from others even when interacting in a simulated virtual test environment where there was no possibility of being infected.[8]

It's possible the pandemic-era rules around personal space created further problems for children who were already struggling with this nonverbal channel. One of the key ways in which children learn the rules of personal space (as well as other nonverbal skills) is through trial and error, and when spatial boundaries are strictly delineated and enforced—as they were during the pandemic—children have fewer opportunities to practice and learn those rules on their own. It's not clear if pandemic-enforced rules will impact children's perceptions about what constitutes an appropriate amount of personal space over the long run, but what we do know is that they will have to learn (or relearn) how to identify and respect their own special boundaries—as well as the boundaries of others—in spaces where appropriate distances are *not* explicitly prescribed.

Needless to say, the increasing amount of time spent on screens has not helped our children's understanding and use of personal space. More and more, young people are conducting large portions of their lives in cyberspace, a place that has no physical dimension and gives us erroneous information about space and its parameters. Moreover, with fewer opportunities to learn about, and practice, the appropriate amount of space to leave between themselves and others during actual in-person social interactions, it makes sense that some kids will struggle with understanding personal space boundaries. Not long ago, I was talking with a teacher outside her room in a school hallway when one of her students, a seven-year-old boy, walked in a straight line between us, instead of around us, even though there was plenty of room. After he passed, the teacher called out, "Zeke, where are you supposed to walk when two people are talking?" His response was a vacant and lost expression.

The good news is because most mistakes in personal space are due to a lack of learning or experience, they can typically be corrected easily. In a very practical way, the pandemic-enforced six-foot-rule was an excellent example of how to go about teaching the appropriate use of personal space. For many people, personal space bubbles became visible for the first time, and we quickly learned new ways of interacting with one another by actively adjusting them. If your child is struggling with personal space boundaries, you can help by explicitly demonstrating the correct space to leave between her own body and those of others.

PERSONAL SPACE IN INFANCY AND EARLY CHILDHOOD

At what point do babies develop an awareness of personal space? One answer comes from psychologist Thomas Horner, who looked closely at how infants reacted to strangers during the first year of their lives. Up to around six months of age, children typically react to hovering and cheek-pinching strangers positively and indiscriminately—and without apparent fear. However, around six months, a change occurs, and children begin to be more wary of strangers, even reacting with distress to some, especially when the stranger controls the interaction and intrudes into the child's personal space. It's during this transition age that, as Dr. Horner puts it, infants become like customs inspectors trying to discern if someone is about to bring illegal goods into their country.[9] Another study conducted by psychologists in Birmingham, England, found that a peripersonal neuron system already exists to some degree even in newborn babies. While there is some debate around when exactly that system becomes operable, there is strong evidence to suggest that at six months, babies begin to develop an observational self, which allows them to both discern who is entering their personal space and determine the potential threat of that person.[10]

For that reason, as babies approach the six-month mark, parents need to be judicious about the kinds of interactions they allow their infants to have and the spatial area within which those interactions take place. Too often I've observed well-intentioned adults intruding into the intimate zone when introducing themselves to a child, even taking the child's hand or hugging them without warning or permission. Adults—and especially adults who are strangers to the child—must take care to respect that space, rather than invade it. At this age, children need to feel safe with someone before inviting them to share their space.

No wonder, then, that infants cling to caregivers and toddlers will only make brief forays away before returning quickly to the safety of their parents' bubble. Slowly but surely, and with the guidance of parents, children begin to venture farther and begin to learn the appropriate distance to keep both from adults they know and from strangers. At the same time, they start to develop a reflexive response to someone coming too close for comfort. Research shows that when infants and young children feel secure in the presence of their caregivers, they are more likely to explore their environments, including the people that inhabit them, which gives them opportunities to learn about the nuances of personal space that will prepare them for future social interactions. In fact, researchers from Israel found that children who trusted their caregivers more in infancy not only tended to be more intrepid explorers; they were also more resistant to intrusions from others, less likely to allow unwanted others into their personal space, and more interpersonally competent a decade later.[11]

For parents, teaching basic use of personal space is a study in patience and active modeling. Keep in mind that the younger the child, the more likely it is that she will keep a similar distance from most anyone, whether a stranger or a family member. That will change as she moves toward the end of early childhood and gains exposure to a broader range of people and interactions.

TIPS FOR MAKING PERSONAL SPACE VISIBLE AND CONCRETE FOR YOUR VERY YOUNG CHILD

1. Talk about personal space bubbles with your child.

You can explain to her that everyone has a space bubble and that it's important to respect those of others. When in public spaces, warn your child not to crash into people and help her become more aware of the people around her.

2. Make your child's space bubble visible and concrete.

You can mark a four-foot-by-four-foot space around your child on the floor using colorful masking tape to help her understand the parameters of her space bubble. Alternatively, if you have a hula hoop, you can get your child to step inside the hoop and walk around carrying it.

3. Play green light / red light.

Green light /red light is a great game to play to help make children aware of one another's personal space (green light means move closer; red light means stop). If you don't have a group of children to play with, you could replicate the game using toy cars, showing how each car needs space around it to travel safely, and that drivers need to follow the rules of green light and red light so they don't crash. (Good training also for fifteen years later when your child needs to learn to drive!)

4. Learn to respect your child's own personal space.

Your child is a growing individual who needs to have some control over who appears in her space and how close people are allowed to be. A lot of adults — including parents and close family members — don't appreciate the importance of allowing a child to decide who gets to enter her personal space. Respecting a child's spatial boundaries, even at an early age, instills an important lesson about respecting the spatial boundaries of others.

PERSONAL SPACE IN LATE CHILDHOOD

Around the time your child begins full-time school, she will have to become much more adept in understanding the rules of personal space. She'll need to know how far to stand from others while waiting in line, when it's appropriate to come close to a friend in the schoolyard, and when it's not. It's quite normal for children to struggle with these boundaries at first—and in different ways. One child may hug others without permission, while another might be prone to unwittingly bumping into peers. One may intrude on a group of classmates by wedging himself into their circle, while another might sit too far away from his lunch companion at the cafeteria table.

Research published from my lab, as well as others, shows that by the age of six, most children have become quite discerning about whom they let into their bubble and whom they keep out. Typically, at this age, children will allow peers of the same sex closer to them than those of the opposite sex, but two girls are generally comfortable with less space between them than two boys are.[12] But for the majority of children at this age, the peripersonal neurons start firing whenever someone approaches them. That's why older children who continue to violate the space of peers are more likely to be rejected socially. While a five-year-old can move in close to play next to another child without consequence, that may not be an acceptable action for a seven-year-old. And by around ten years of age, children will be expected to follow rules as if they were adults.

When children are able to confidently navigate personal space boundaries, they have a much easier time making and maintaining friendships — and not just because their peers are less likely to reject them. Space is the way we communicate closeness, not only physically but socially as well. As such, it plays a role in all four stages of any relationship, though its role is particularly significant when *initiating* and *deepening* relationships. Once a child is ready to initiate a possible relationship with another child, she will need to maintain the correct distance in order for the new friend to see her facial expressions and hear her words, but not be so close that her overture is seen as intrusive.

Imagine a young boy — let's call him Austin — playing on the playground during recess on the first day at a new school. He sees a classmate prodding something on the ground with a stick. He walks over. Austin stands at a slight distance, as he doesn't know the other child yet.

"What is it?" he calls out.

"A really big, strange bug," the other boy replies.

"Can I see it?" Austin requests.

"Sure, but be careful," the other boy cautions.

Now that the other boy has invited Austin into his personal space, Austin moves closer.

"Wow, I've never seen anything like that before," he tells the other boy.

As the two boys observe the bug, standing almost shoulder to shoulder, a friendship has been initiated based on a shared interest. The boys soon learn each other's names and, later in the day, discover they both enjoy playing basketball after school.

Although Austin's behavior may not seem all that noteworthy, in fact, he's done a great job navigating personal space to successfully initiate a new relationship. He asked permission before approaching, then closed the space slowly, giving the other boy time to become comfortable with his approach, and at the end of it all they stood comfortably together, ready to get to know each other better. Imagine how different it might have been if Austin had run over and immediately sidled up beside the other boy with no regard for his personal space boundaries.

When two people reduce the space between them — as Austin and his new friend did — they create the conditions for the relationship to deepen. Because almost all nonverbal communication — including facial expressions, postures, gestures, and so on — takes place within the intimate and personal zones, two children who can share this space comfortably have access to nonverbal information from each other that others don't. This is how children can form that "chum" relationship Harry Stack Sullivan wrote about: a special friendship in which children learn to share secrets, trust each other's opinion, and hone their interpersonal skills.

Children who learn to master these foundational rules in late childhood will be that much better prepared to navigate the future (and often sexualized) relationships of adolescence, where personal space errors can have far more negative consequences. In other words, it's never too early to teach your child about how to navigate personal space.

TIPS FOR HELPING CHILDREN NAVIGATE PERSONAL SPACE DURING LATE CHILDHOOD

1. Observe your child in a variety of social situations.

Parents are often unaware when their school-age child has problems with personal space, as space bubbles are generally much smaller at home with family members. It's important, therefore, to observe your child in different situations and settings. Note how far away she stands from others depending on where she is and with whom she's interacting. Does she modify appropriately depending on the type of relationship, moving closer with friends and farther away with strangers?

2. Continue to give your child feedback.

Compliment your child when he is mindful of the space of others, and gently redirect him when he oversteps boundaries: "I like how you went up to your new friend and stood a nice distance away from him before asking him if he wanted to play." "It's not good to bump into people when you're playing with them. It's better to give your friends space."

3. **Gradually give your child more freedom to explore her world.**

    In spaces where it is safe to do so, let your child wander off while letting her know how far she can (and can't) go and showing that you'll be in the same spot waiting for her when she returns. If your child moves too far away from you too soon, you may feel you need to reprimand her, but if the reprimands are too severe or, on the other hand, if she is permitted to stray without parental feedback, she will miss out on valuable opportunities to learn the rules for personal space.

4. **Ask your child to be a "personal space bubble detective."**

    When you are out with your child in public places you can ask her to observe people standing at different distances from one another and have her tell you what's happening. Do the people know one another? Do they like one another? Do you think they are friends? Family members? While watching people standing in line, see how far they stand from one another—this is another great opportunity to observe personal space rules in action.

5. **Have your child walk toward you and then use facial expressions and gestures to show her when it's time to stop.**

    This is a good way to teach your child how to observe personal space rules, while also reinforcing other nonverbal skills.

You can also reverse roles and get your child to signal when she wants you to stop. Children need to become aware of how nonverbal cues in facial expressions, tones of voice, postures, and gestures can be useful signals of unwelcome personal space intrusions.

6. Make time to have a conversation about consent.

Ask your child if she has ever been made uncomfortable by someone being too close. Reassure her that she has the right to tell others to stop getting closer when she is made uncomfortable by the approach. Children need to acquire both the nonverbal *and* verbal language to negotiate personal space interactions. If she has trouble asserting her boundaries — or asking others about theirs — have her practice phrases like, "You're in my space, please move back," or "Is it okay if I come close to look at what you're doing?"

7. Teach your child about the difference between the intimate, personal, social, and public zones.

Explain that you can say personal things in the intimate zone that you wouldn't say in the other zones and redirect him if, for example, he shouts across a room to discuss an intimate topic. I remember one ten-year-old who wanted to be friends with another child and decided to show his concern for this classmate by shouting loudly across the room, "How's your diarrhea?" Well-meaning and perhaps empathetic — but also a sure way to embarrass and push away a potential friend.

8. **Teach your child how to navigate space when inside an elevator.**

Explain to her that when someone enters the elevator, she should step aside if she can in order to give that person space. This is a great way to help your child practice adjusting her space bubble even in a cramped environment.

9. **Observe Personal Space Day, which is celebrated on November 30.**

Yes! Personal Space Day exists, and it may provide an opportunity for you and your child to pause and reflect on the importance of respecting the personal boundaries of others.

WHEN YOUR CHILD NEEDS EXPERT INTERVENTION

The nonverbal channel of personal space becomes ever more important as your child grows older. Early childhood and especially the transition to full-time school are crucial times to identify and correct skill gaps before they become more extensive and harmful. If your child is persistently struggling with spatial awareness, it's likely your child's teacher will bring it to your attention. If your child continues to make the same errors, even after teachers repeatedly correct her, you may decide to have her formally assessed by a clinical psychologist or learning disability specialist with experience in personal space preferences and behavior.

PERSONAL SPACE

* * * * * *

MISUSING PERSONAL SPACE always impedes the development of relationships, but its impacts pale in comparison to the social difficulties that can arise when children (or adults) make mistakes using touch. As you will see in the next chapter, touch can carry more emotional information than any other nonverbal channel—which means it's all the more imperative for young people to get it right.

CHAPTER 6

Physical Touch

Proceed with Caution

As I write this I am glancing up at framed photographs of my wife and granddaughter. In my wife's photo, she is looking at me with a smile that instantly conjures her presence, as if she was right there in the room with me. In the photo of my then two-month-old granddaughter, Hannah Ruth, she is lying facedown on my chest while I lean back in my recliner, with her head resting over my heart. These photos remind me of the powerful lessons my granddaughter and wife taught me about the importance of touch during one of the lowest times in my life.

Late one summer evening in 2002, as my wife and I were getting ready to return home from a trip to England, I had a heart attack. After being stabilized in an English hospital, I returned home to Atlanta to find out I would have to have major bypass surgery. I met with my surgeon, who happened to be one of my past students — one of my very brightest students, I might add — who explained what was going to happen during the operation. He could tell I was shaken by what had happened and scared about what would happen next and asked if there was anything he could say or do to allay my fears. I shared an idea I had been considering. Would he let me take a small photograph of my wife with me into preop? He smiled and said he didn't see why not. So, on the day of the surgery, as they prepared me for what would turn out to be a quadruple bypass operation, I clutched and was calmed by the photo of someone I loved.

As it turns out, I was onto something; research done since then has shown that the presence of and touch from someone you care for can lessen your experience of pain.[1] In one interesting experiment, psychologists tested people experiencing pain while alone, while holding the hand of someone they didn't know well, and while holding the hand of someone for whom they cared. They found that holding the hand of someone for whom they cared not only produced brain patterns that were in synch but also led to feeling less pain.[2] There is even one study showing that hugs can reduce the occurrence of upper respiratory illness and the severity of symptoms of those infected.[3] The benefits of touch, I would argue, are incontrovertible, especially for young children who crave reassurance or safety.

As I was recovering from my surgery, my granddaughter Hannah Ruth was born, initiating me into the unique and wonderful world of being a grandfather (or Pappah, as I would come to be called). My recovery was a difficult one. My chest hurt constantly, and I had trouble sleeping. The only time I could rest easily was when I had my lovely new granddaughter lying on my chest; her touch was like a salve—literally and figuratively—for my heart. She wasn't the best of sleepers either, but when she was cradled in my arms, we both nodded off almost immediately. Every time I look at those two photos on my desk, I'm reminded about the unique power of human touch to soothe, nurture, and heal.

Touch is among the most emotionally powerful channels of nonverbal communication—one that is central to our human experience from infancy and throughout our lifetimes. It's difficult to imagine a world in which we couldn't hold and cuddle our newborns and have a ready supply of hugs for our toddlers' falls and disappointments. As adults, touch remains central to our own sense of well-being; think of the power of a squeeze of a hand or an arm around the shoulders reassuring us that we are not alone. While other nonverbal behaviors can take place virtually (albeit in a distorted form), touch *must* happen in the actual, physical world, where it is impossible to touch without being touched back. In the previous chapter, I discussed the personal space that exists around us to warn us of outside threats. Touch can occur only when we allow someone into that space—or they allow us into theirs—and in order to do so we must trust that the other person wishes to express caring rather than harm.

Communications involving touch can be both physically and emotionally powerful. They can also be extraordinarily complex. The number of messages we can convey through physical touch is vast. We can poke, pat, stroke, caress, slap, hug, grip, hit, rub, kiss, squeeze, tickle, scratch, grab (and much more), each one with a different meaning. And to complicate matters further, that meaning can depend on the timing, intensity, duration, and context of the touch. Touch can be nurturing, and it can be threatening. It can be social, romantic, or sexual. The main focus of this chapter, however, is on social touch, the kind that is nonsexual and well-meaning and carries emotional messages that connect us to others, such as a handshake or high five, a hand on a shoulder or arm, a quick hug, a peck on the cheek, squeezing or holding a hand, and an arm around the shoulders or linked in another person's arm.

WHY TOUCH MATTERS

In the prior chapter, I wrote about the peripersonal neurons that are triggered when our space is broached. Not to be outdone, touch also has its own specially designed neural cells, called C-touch fibers. These cells can carry an amazing number of emotional messages depending on the kinds of touch received and the situations in which the touch takes place. C-touch fibers have a much more complex role to play compared to the simple threat that triggers peripersonal neurons.[4] In fact, different C-touch fibers have different neural connections, which allow them to communicate more nuanced emotional messages, in an intricate operation that psychologist

Carissa Cascio and her colleagues described eloquently as "that of a musical chord comprising individual notes on a keyboard that when struck, a pure note ensues, but combinations of individual keys produce chords that are more than the sum of their parts."[5] There's even a unique connection between certain C-touch fibers and other nervous system functions, like the zygomatic nerve, which controls our smiles. This may explain why we smile when we get that sympathetic peck on the cheek from a loved one after a stressful day of work or when we get an enthusiastic high five from a colleague for a job well done.

When used appropriately, touch can be powerfully reassuring when we are sad and wonderfully affirming when we are happy. In a now-classic study, psychologist April Crusco and her colleagues investigated the effect of touch by instructing one group of waitresses to touch customers lightly on the hand when returning their change, and another group of waitresses not to touch the customers at all. It turned out that customers who had experienced the physical contact gave larger tips than those who hadn't, regardless of the gender of the customer, the atmosphere of the restaurant, or the dining experience.[6] In similar studies, library patrons who were touched lightly on the hand by librarians at checkout indicated they liked the library more than those who were not, people passing by a store counter were more likely to try a new product if touched by the staff lightly on the arm, and students who were touched in the same manner by teachers were more likely to volunteer during class.[7]

Studies show that the nonverbal channel of touch is absolutely crucial to a child's development at every phase. One of the first psychologists to study its importance was Harry Harlow. Back in the 1950s, he set about trying to answer the question of why infant mammals cling to their mothers. In that era, the assumption was that infants stayed close to their mothers because they needed them for food and sustenance. Through studying infant monkeys, Harlow learned that when given the choice of a soft, fuzzy doll in the shape of a mother or a mother figure made of wood and wire, the young monkeys preferred the fuzzy mother surrogate, even when offered food or a bottle of milk if they chose the wood and wire version. The infant monkeys, it seemed, craved the soft, nurturing touch more even than the sustenance of food and drink. A few decades later we were able to obtain human data that supported Harlow's findings and confirmed the importance of maternal touch and nurturance in the healthy development of infants.[8]

More recently, the pandemic has made it clear to all of us just how central the nonverbal channel of touch is to our sense of well-being. We could have guessed how emotionally difficult it would be not to be able to hold the hand of a dying parent or open our arms to embrace others who were frightened or grieving, but many of us were unprepared for how much it hurt to refrain from greeting a friend with a hug or extending a warm handshake to a coworker once the social restrictions of lockdown were eased. For me, like most every grandparent in the world, not being able to pull my grandchildren into a giant bear hug was pure torture.

PHYSICAL TOUCH

Touch is the way we express affection and care for others at every stage of our lives. We might deepen a friendship through affectionate squeezes or by linking arms when walking, or by marking milestones such as birthdays, marriages, or graduations with high fives and hugs. But touch is important even at the very beginning of a relationship. Greeting someone with a firm, polite handshake on first meeting can set a positive tone for the entire interaction, and handshakes held an extra moment or two, with a touch on the arm at the same time, can signal a deepening of a relationship just as much as any spoken communication or hug.

OF COURSE, TOUCH can also be used in ways that are aggressive or entirely inappropriate. From a young age, most of us learn that punching, hitting, pinching, pushing, scratching, biting, and slapping are not allowed, that certain private parts of the body are off-limits for touching in social situations, or under any circumstances. Moreover, the rules and norms around what constitutes appropriate touch depend on a variety of factors, including how well we know the other person, the setting or situation, the other person's expectations (for example, they are expecting a handshake and we go in for a hug, and vice versa), and more.

Touch is the most-high stakes nonverbal channel in this respect, as mistakes can have severe consequences beyond social difficulties, especially as children enter adolescence, at which point the penalty for inappropriate touching can even include legal punishment. Touch is also the only nonverbal channel for which children are explicitly taught some hard-and-fast rules, such as not touching private parts—although these kinds of dictates are much easier to teach than more subtle, nebulous rules, such as how to tap someone on the shoulder when approaching them from behind (in case you're wondering, it's best to do it with one finger, gently, touching a one-square-inch area midway between the shoulder and the neck).

To add to this complexity, the etiquette around touch is different in different parts of the world. For example, in countries like Spain and Italy, people favor a lot more social touching than in other cultures, and it's perfectly acceptable for people who have only just met to hug and kiss on the cheek to say hello. In the United States and United Kingdom—two of the least "touch-friendly" countries in the world—any form of touch other than a quick handshake is taboo in most educational and professional environments. In America we favor the very firm handshake, but in some cultures a softer handshake is considered more appropriate. Despite these substantial differences, findings from a recent survey of more than thirteen hundred participants from Finland, France, Italy, Russia, and the United Kingdom reveal that country and culture are not the main drivers of norms and behaviors when it comes to touch. Instead, it's the closeness of the relationship between the two people involved. Like all nonverbal behavior, the meaning of social touch varies depending on our relationship with the other person. If I accidentally brush hands with a stranger in a crowd, that may be interpreted very differently than if I brush hands affectionately with my wife. Accordingly, a child who is used to giving his siblings big, long squeezes at home may find that children at his preschool don't enjoy being hugged with quite the same enthusiasm.[9]

There's no doubt that children who don't follow basic touch rules may find themselves alienating their peers. Third grade was a long time ago for me, but I can still remember my classmate Jenny, and how I was always upset when I was assigned to a group project alongside her or forced to play with her. The reason was simple: she couldn't keep her hands to herself. Jenny appeared to have an almost compulsive need to touch things. If she wasn't rubbing her arms or running the fabric of her dress between her fingers, she was touching others, even when it was clear that they didn't welcome it. More than a few times, this resulted in some altercation—such as the time she snuck up behind a classmate and began playing with her long, silky hair so vigorously that she managed to tug at it, hurting the other girl in the process. I remember thinking that Jenny really did look sorry afterward and promised to keep her hands to herself.

Although Jenny's behavior was certainly annoying to her classmates, I also remember the ways that touch was used positively in the classroom. When Jenny was behaving inappropriately, our teacher, Mrs. Harris, would come by Jenny's desk, gently placing her hand on the back of her shoulder for a brief moment to help calm her down. Mrs. Harris used the nonverbal channel of touch in other ways as well. She held children's hands during recess, and if two kids were fighting, she would step in between them and hold them apart until they quieted down. Hugs were plentiful and appreciated in her classroom, whether as an expression of joy or a means of consoling a crying child. The small gestures of contact made my classmates and me feel safe, reassured, and part of a community. They also, as I later came to understand, gave us a model for how to use touch appropriately. Mrs. Harris's approach has since been affirmed by Swedish psychologists Disa Bergnehr and Asta Cekaite, who completed one of the few studies on the impact of touch behavior in preschool classes and found that hugging, placing hands on a child's arm, and other forms of appropriate touch on the part of the teacher were an effective means of both keeping order during class activities and showing fondness for the children in their care.[10]

Much has changed in our American classrooms since my days as a third grader. In most educational institutions across the country, teachers are more or less forbidden from touching their students in any way, shape, or form (as are coaches, youth group leaders, and pretty much every adult other than a child's own family members). Classmates must also refrain from touching each other, except in tightly controlled situations. Pervasive concern about sexual and physical abuse — along with the possible legal ramifications that might result from inappropriate touching — have led to the theory that it's better not to touch anyone at all in classrooms than to risk getting it wrong.

While these fears are understandable, the blanket ban on touching has also produced an unintended consequence: children no longer have opportunities to learn the intricate rules of appropriate social touch from a trusted adult or peer who is not a family member. Despite strong recommendations from psychologists and educators who understand that young children require such experiences at this time in their lives to prepare them for adolescence and beyond, our classrooms have become strict touch-free zones. Instead of showing children the many ways that touch can be used appropriately to calm, comfort, and connect, as Mrs. Harris did with Jenny, teachers have taken on the role of "touch police." When I once asked a ten-year-old boy who was having social interaction difficulties in school what he knew about touch, he first looked at the floor and then at the ceiling, and then finally turned to me and said, quietly but intensely, "Don't touch!"

Although touch was already largely forbidden in the school setting by 2020, the pandemic made things worse. Initially seen as a possible vehicle for virus transmission, our touch behavior became modified down to nil, as six-foot social distancing rules became the norm. Since then, most of us have returned to our usual handshakes and hugs, but the reality is that our children lost two years' worth of practice in learning how to use touch to communicate their affection or their wish for more closeness in a budding friendship. Laura Crucianelli, a neuroscientist at the Karolinska Institute in Stockholm, has argued that rebuilding these skills should be a priority in the post-pandemic new normal. She suggested that by depriving ourselves of touch, we lose access to one of the most sophisticated and important ways to communicate and along with that the opportunities to build new relationships.[11]

The evidence is clear that nothing can replace the comfort a child gets from someone holding their hand when they're scared, hugging them when they're sad, or putting an arm around their shoulders to show affection or support. We should all be concerned about how the lack of physical contact impacts children emotionally, as well as developmentally. And while the risk of inappropriate contact from teachers and peers should be taken seriously, we must also recognize that one of the best ways to keep children safe from abuse is by teaching them about the nuances of appropriate touch at a young age.

David Linden, author of *Touch: The Science of the Hand, Heart, and Mind,* points out that we are born with touch sensitivity that increases until around age twenty and then drops about 1 percent each year after that. In other words, children's sense of touch is developing dramatically during early and late childhood, meaning that we have a short window to help them understand and utilize the subtleties of touch before adolescence sets in and complications of romantic and sexualized touch come into play.[12]

With teachers prohibited from modeling appropriate social touch for children in the classroom, parents must step in to fill this large gap in children's nonverbal education and ensure their children receive the knowledge and skill they are presently missing. This chapter will help you do that.

TOUCH IN INFANCY AND EARLY CHILDHOOD

Even before your child is born, he will begin to use his sense of touch to explore his world and build relationships. Scientists believe that the C-touch fibers are already in operation prenatally in the third trimester, because when mothers touch their abdomen, fetuses respond with more tactile activity of their own on the uterine wall.[13] Most infants, once born, have endless amounts of physical contact with caregivers, most often from mothers instinctively stroking their infants at the speed necessary to stimulate their C-touch fibers. As for the rest of us, we usually don't need to be persuaded. Parents, grandparents, aunts, uncles, cousins, friends, alike: everyone loves to cuddle the baby.

As your child grows, he gets to know textures by using what's known as "discriminatory touch," which allows him to distinguish between the warm, smooth skin of a parent and the soft fleece of a blanket. He begins to understand the emotions associated with touch, such as when someone rubs his back or gives a hug, a type of touch known as "affective touch."

Your child's C-touch fibers communicate with a complex array of neural systems responsible for the development of what's known as the "social brain." Francis McGlone, a professor in neuroscience at Liverpool John Moores University in the United Kingdom and a leader in the field of affective touch, calls C-touch fibers the missing aspect that glues everything social together.[14] Without touch, the system in the brain responsible for social interactions and behavior will fail to mature properly, which may result in low emotional sensitivity and a loss of interest in others — struggles that can last a lifetime.

Most everyone agrees that infants need a great deal of nurturant touch to form secure attachments and develop emotionally. In one stark example of this, when a team of American psychologists were brought in to observe Romanian children who had spent time in warehouse orphanages during the leadership of Nicolae Ceaușescu in the 1980s — referred to by some as "child gulags" because of the unspeakable conditions and neglect these abandoned children were forced to endure — they were stunned to find the rooms filled with infants who were eerily quiet. Meanwhile, older children walked around zombielike, with blank facial expressions; some rocked endlessly, while others punched themselves, screamed, or banged their heads against the wall. Most were socially withdrawn and would not speak. These children had been almost entirely deprived of physical contact and suffered severe cognitive and emotional deficits as a result. They couldn't process emotion nonverbally by reading faces, they didn't respond to communication via touch or reassuring voices, and they seemed uninterested in any kind of contact with others. Subsequent neuroimaging studies found that their brains had not sufficiently developed in regions that support attention, general cognition, and emotional and sensory processing.[15]

Once the plight of the children was brought to the attention of the public, programs were initiated in an attempt to reverse these social and emotional deficits. Thankfully, follow-up studies have since found that the longer the children spent in the care of their adoptive parents or nurturing caregivers, the greater was the likelihood their emotional processing deficiencies could be reversed through healthy, loving touch and nurturing human connection.[16]

At around eight months—at roughly the same time babies become more discriminating about whom they allow into their personal space—most infants will, much like the infant monkeys in Harlow's study, become attached to some soft object, like a cloth blanket or furry animal that they carry with them everywhere. The familiar textures and smells of these objects provide comfort when little ones are apart from parents and caregivers. As babies become more mobile, first crawling and then toddling, the amount of time spent in the arms of a parent or caregiver naturally decreases, but touch is still a major component of their daily lives. It's only when they arrive at day care or the preschool classroom that the amount of affective touch they receive begins to decrease significantly and continues to decrease over time.

TIPS FOR INTRODUCING YOUR VERY YOUNG CHILD TO THE NUANCES OF TOUCH

1. Get to know your child's touch style.

You can spend time observing the many ways your very young child interacts with the world using touch. Some little children are touch seekers—they want to touch everything and everyone in sight—while some are touch avoiders. Some kids are clingy; some prefer to be more independent. Very young children will have different styles, and by observing them in action, you can better support them as they learn to use touch in their day-to-day life. While it is perfectly normal for styles to differ from child to child, a touch-seeking child will likely need to be redirected so he doesn't overstep boundaries with others, while a touch-avoiding child will likely need encouragement to make contact in appropriate situations, but he should never be forced.

2. **Be aware of how your child's gender may affect your own touch style.**

    In our culture, we've been socialized to treat infants and toddlers in different ways depending on their gender, and this often includes treating little girls gently—like delicate vases that could shatter at our touch—while little boys generally receive more energetic tickling, roughhousing, and bouncing on laps. Keep in mind that boys may crave those gentle back rubs just as much as their sisters do. And girls may want to be bounced on knees or thrown up in the air just as much as their brothers.

3. **Teach your child about the power of positive (and negative) touch.**

    Even when your child is still learning to walk and talk, you can teach through gentle direction and affirmation that pokes, prods, pinches, and hitting are not allowed, but that hugs and holding hands with friends are just fine—as long as the friend also wants to hug and hold hands back. If your child does make a mistake and touches inappropriately, you can use this as a teaching opportunity.

4. Give your child authority over his own body.

Just as you taught your child that he has authority over who is allowed to enter his personal space, you can teach your child that he doesn't have to touch someone or be touched by someone if he doesn't want to—and that if he doesn't want to hug a close relative or friend, it's okay to say no. Encourage friends and relatives to ask permission, as in "May I hold your hand while we walk to the playground?" or "Is it okay if I give you a hug?" If he prefers not to express affection in this way, you can suggest he blow the friend or family member a kiss—from a comfortable distance—instead. As soon as your child begins to talk, you can give him the language to talk about how he wants to be touched (or not). You can practice phrases with him such as "Please stop"; "Don't touch my hair—I don't like it"; "Could you hold my hand? I'm scared."

5. After your child begins day care and preschool, make time to be physically affectionate with your child after school.

In today's day cares and preschool classrooms, even very young children aren't given very much physical affection during the day. As a busy parent, it's important to take every opportunity to make up for this deficit when your young child is at home with you. This doesn't mean you have to hug him constantly. You can sit right next to him, with the sides of your bodies touching, even if he isn't on your lap, put your arm around him when reading a book, have fun with tickles at bath time, and of course cuddles at bedtime. This example will help your child learn about different ways to be physically affectionate that are welcomed and appropriate within families.

6. Don't reprimand or punish your child for self-soothing.

One of the ways very young children respond to a lack of touch during the day is by self-soothing. Children may suck thumbs, twist and chew hair, or even play with genitals. If this happens, it's important to understand why children are displaying these behaviors: in most cases, they are simply craving the reassurance of touch. As a parent, it's important not to freak out at, shame, or punish your child for self-soothing. The best way to deal with this normal behavior is to redirect your child, providing the distraction of another more appropriate way to soothe, such as giving him a toy to hug or a tactile game to play.

7. Start to have the "good touch, bad touch" talk with your child, even at this early age.

Experts suggest that these discussions begin during the preschool years and continue through the transition to full-time elementary school and throughout childhood. You can begin with a simple lesson about the names of body parts using anatomically correct names. Then you can talk with your child about which body parts are private. Tell your child to imagine a swimsuit or swim trunks and explain that the parts that are covered by the swimwear are private and should not be touched.

You can look in a mirror and ask your child to point to different body parts as she looks at her reflection or use a doll to show her areas that are off-limits. As children get older, you can return to this topic and continue to reinforce it in age-appropriate ways.

TOUCH IN LATE CHILDHOOD

Although infants receive plenty of touch from the adults around them during infancy, they get progressively less as they approach late childhood, when they face the daunting task of beginning kindergarten and elementary school—one of the most important social developmental periods in their lives. All your child's nonverbal skills are needed if he is going to succeed in this transition, but because touch is the only nonverbal channel whose use is actively prohibited in classrooms, you as the parent will have to put more emphasis on guiding your child in this area.

TOUCH IN THE CLASSROOM

Back in 2011, teachers Pamela Owen and Jonathan Gillentine sent surveys to K through third-grade teachers to find out how they felt about positive touch in classrooms and how they were using this particular nonverbal channel with their students. The results of the survey were clear: more than 90 percent of teachers believed positive touch enhances emotional development, shows caring, improves mood, and reduces stress in classrooms. Yet fewer than half of these same teachers actually used touch with their students when they had the opportunity.[17]

Along with many preschool and elementary school educators, I'm an advocate for allowing positive touch back into our classrooms so that young children can learn about how to touch in a safe and structured way. If you agree, you may want to raise this important issue with your child's teachers and school administrators. As a first step, you could present some of the latest findings around touch in classrooms such as the Swedish study I've cited in this chapter about the effectiveness of touch in education. You could offer to lend them a copy of this book and ask them to read this chapter as a way to begin a discussion around reinstituting positive touch. You could also suggest inviting a psychologist, counselor, or other qualified professional to speak with educators and other families about this topic.

My three suggestions for school administrators and teachers who are interested in changing the "touch" culture of our preschools and elementary schools are as follows:

1. Include parents and caregivers.

It's always best if administrators and educators can include parents and caregivers in setting up new standards for the classroom. Once there are clear and defined rules on touch that everyone is aware of, these policies need to be reviewed and refreshed with children and families throughout the school year.

2. Set parameters for how and when touch takes place.

Whenever possible, teachers and childcare workers should ensure that touch takes place only in the presence of other colleagues. Teachers and childcare workers should ask children before any physical contact is initiated.

3. **Make touch part of the curriculum.**

Teaching children about this important nonverbal channel should become part of the curriculum, with teachers explaining the difference between appropriate and inappropriate touch, the negative effects of hitting, biting, and pinching, and the positive effects of kind and respectful social touch.

TIPS FOR ENCOURAGING POSITIVE TOUCH IN LATE CHILDHOOD

1. **Continue to observe your child's touching style.**

Spend time observing your child as he interacts with his peers. Is he using touch to successfully foster new connections or is he inadvertently alienating other children? Does he hang all over another child even though the child is indicating by words and facial expressions that this is unwelcome? Does he try to grab and hold a peer's hand while walking without asking for permission and ignore the plea to "let go"? Take time to observe if, on the other hand, he is avoiding the appropriate touch advances of others. When he and his friends meet others and exchange hugs, does he shrink away and look pained or become rigid and unresponsive? Once you have made these observations, you will be in a better position to encourage and redirect your child.

2. **Enroll your child in sports teams or classes that have some element of touch in them.**

Martial arts, basketball, dance, football, or even "no-touch" sports such as soccer that will still have touch rituals such as pregame handshakes and fist bumps are all good options. In these controlled environments, children will have opportunities to navigate touch in ways that are structured and appropriate.

3. **Never forget the power of a gentle touch to soothe or encourage your child when he is anxious.**

If your child is standing nervously on the threshold of a new classroom or social situation, then you can touch him lightly on the back of the shoulder as he walks in. If your child is struggling with a homework assignment, you can sit next to him with knees touching as you help him complete it. If he is scared of the dentist or doctor, ask if you can hold his hand during the appointment. Physical closeness to you will release signals via his C-touch fibers, reassuring him that he is safe. Even the briefest or most fleeting moment of contact can make a difference.

4. **Teach your school-age child about how to shake hands.**

The handshake is an appropriate form of social touch that will serve your child well in adulthood. Show him how to extend a hand at the right angle and grasp firmly but not tightly when shaking, while looking the other person in the eye. You can also explain to your child that while this is the convention in America, not every culture uses the handshake. You can tell him that if he ever feels unsure as to what to do, he can wait for the other person to make the greeting and then mimic that.

5. **As your child gets older, you can return to the "good touch, bad touch" conversation.**

Remind him of the basics, answer any questions he might have, and generally refresh the topic. Continue to remind him of his authority over his own body, and support him when he doesn't want physical contact, even if it's from another family member.

6. **Sit down with your child and make a simple list of rules for physical touch that can be posted on a refrigerator or bulletin board.**

As a parent, it's important to make rules around touch explicit, or your child will likely have to learn the hard way if he oversteps a boundary at school. It's a good idea to use basic language to make the rules concrete and understandable. Remind him that anything covered by a bathing suit is considered off-limits for touching, and that touching others anywhere else should be brief and soft unless it is part of a monitored sport or game. Demonstrate or perhaps provide a drawing showing how to touch someone when approaching from behind (with one finger, touching softly in a small area midway between the neck and the shoulder). If your child does make a mistake and uses touch in ways that are inappropriate, you can turn this into an opportunity to review the rules around touching and then teach him about the importance of making amends. You can suggest your child apologize either in person or by writing a note.

WHEN YOUR CHILD NEEDS EXPERT INTERVENTION

If you as a parent feel that your child has suddenly become hypersensitive to touch, you should start by communicating with your pediatrician first to be sure physical illness or allergies are not the cause. For some children who have this hypersensitivity, clothing, food textures, brushing of teeth, or hugs can be unpleasant or even painful. If the hypersensitivity doesn't seem to have a physical cause, it's possible your child would benefit from meeting with an occupational therapist, who will undertake a formal evaluation and perhaps suggest therapeutic activities, most of which involve helping children get used to different types and pressures of touch. In the meantime, you can be helpful by warning your touch-resistant child when they are about to be touched, and by touching them somewhat firmly if needed—being touched lightly is often more repellent to hypersensitive children than a firm touch—and never tickling. If your child is getting into trouble at school because he is a "touch seeker," you may want to have him evaluated and work with your child's teacher to find appropriate ways to redirect him in class.

PHYSICAL TOUCH

· · · · · ·

BECAUSE TOUCH IS the only nonverbal channel in which physical contact is a necessity, it is one that is relatively easy to demonstrate and observe. Our next channel, vocalics, is more difficult to pin down because it hides in and among the words we use. However, our children must master its use in order to connect with others in meaningful ways.

CHAPTER 7

Vocalics

Can You Hear What My Words Aren't Saying?

IN HIS MID-THIRTIES AND DRESSED SMARTLY IN AN EXPENSIVE-looking suit, Ben greeted me with a smile and a warm handshake. As we talked, I remember being impressed by his sense of presence—finding it quite hard to believe his organization had referred him to me for assessment. The problem was that, after a meteoric rise through the company, Ben had hit a brick wall. According to his supervisors, he was a man who most everyone liked and who had been respected by coworkers in his previous positions, but who had seriously botched several recent interactions, not only with coworkers but with prospective clients from other companies as well. Talks with senior partners had not resulted in any improvement, and no one could explain his sudden decline in effectiveness, least of all Ben. I was a last resort before Ben might lose his job.

After our interview and a number of cognitive and personality assessments — including an IQ test, which showed he was of near genius-level intelligence — I began assessing Ben's nonverbal abilities, including the ability to identify emotion in facial expressions, tones of voice, and postures. Consistent with his earlier performance on the cognitive assessments, Ben aced facial expression and postures tests and showed that he understood how personal space should be used and when touch was appropriate. Only one test remained; assuming he also passed this one with flying colors, my report would have to say that I'd found nothing to explain why this man's rise to stardom in his organization had come to such an abrupt halt.

The final test measured the ability to identify emotion in verbal communication: not the words themselves, but the way the words are said. I played Ben several recordings of people saying the same sentence, "I'm going out of the room now, but I'll be back later," while communicating different emotions, and for the first time during our interview, I saw him hesitate and become nervous. He would listen and name an emotion, but then immediately begin to doubt his answer, saying something like, "Well, maybe not, maybe it's..." By the end of this relatively brief test, Ben was so flustered, he looked as if he had just finished running a marathon.

As it turned out, he had reason to be concerned. His scores were comparable to those we would expect of a five-year-old child. Ben was simply unable to pick up and identify the emotion in people's voices, and it was apparent that he, and others around him, were unaware of it. Further questioning revealed why this issue had only become apparent in recent months: his present position was the first one to take him out of the field and into an office setting. In the field he had access to what people were feeling by reading their facial expressions, postures, gestures, and how they occupied the shared space. But now that he was in the office, all of his interactions were taking place by phone. Without the benefit of visual clues, Ben was lost, causing him to miss the nonverbal cues necessary for conversation to flow. Once we identified the problem, Ben's employers had him undertake a program of direct learning and also sent him back out in the field—where soon he was successful again.

WHY VOCALICS MATTER

"Vocalics" is an umbrella term describing everything that we convey with our voices beyond the words themselves: including pitch, tone, volume, and emphasis. The complexity of meaning carried in our voices is extraordinary. In fact, Yale psychologist Michael Kraus has concluded that when it comes to communicating emotion, vocalics is by far the most important of all the nonverbal channels. Based on his research, Kraus goes so far as to suggest that if we want to take the true measure of how someone is feeling, we should probably stop looking at the person and just listen to his or her voice instead. For example, if someone tells you that she's "doing great" in a quiet and trembling voice, we're unlikely to believe her words and much more likely to believe her intonation.[1]

Research shows that there is a strong and consistent association between the ability to identify emotion in voices and social success.[2] When psychologist Alexia Rothman and I constructed the vocalics test that is part of the DANVA, a test that has been used in hundreds of studies to assess children's accuracy in reading cues in the voices of other children and adults, we found that the higher their score, the better their social adjustment and the higher their academic achievement.[3] This remained true even when controlling for cognitive ability, age, sex, and parents' education, according to the research findings of Leonor Neves and her colleagues, published in the *Royal Society Open Science* journal. And as Ben's story demonstrates, if a difficulty with vocalics persists into adulthood, it can undermine not only a person's social success but their career success as well.

Interestingly, the degree to which vocal attributes contribute to our understanding of others goes even beyond just emotions. Scientists have found that if we listen closely to a recording of someone counting out loud from one to ten, we can even guess (at better than chance) the person's age, sex, weight, and general health, as well as native language, region of the country spent as a child, and social status.

VOCALICS

Scientists have traced the origin of our vocalics back some four hundred thousand years to the short, emotional nonverbal sounds made by primates, known as affect bursts. As we evolved into Homo sapiens, our ability to understand the meanings of these sounds, and use them effectively to convey meaning ourselves, gave us an evolutionary advantage. Even before we had language in the form of words, we could pick up signals of distress from children in danger, share warnings, and identify friends from foes. As we evolved further, we began using words with concrete verbal meaning, but we continued to communicate using vocalics, as we had done when we were primates, via the *volume, tone, pitch, rate,* and *emphasis* in our voices.[4]

Words are multitaskers. They carry not only verbal but nonverbal information too. On an average day, most people will hear somewhere between twenty thousand and thirty thousand words.[5] Although we speak at around 150 words a minute, we can listen much faster than we speak, at about 450 words a minute. This leaves us time to process both the verbal content of a person's words and the nonverbal information carried in their vocalics.[6]

Just as personal space depends to some extent on the functioning of the peripersonal neurons and touch on the C-touch fibers, our ability to use vocalics depends on a small but dynamic area of the brain called the superior temporal sulcus. Research using advanced fMRI techniques by psychologist Simon Leipold and his colleagues at Stanford University has found that the superior temporal sulcus becomes more active when we accurately decode emotion in the voices of others. His team revealed it to be a hub for connecting incoming vocalic information with outgoing emotional judgments. Repeated exposure to a range of pitches, tones, and other vocalics alongside accompanying verbal and nonverbal expression of emotions creates the connections through which this part of the brain develops.[7]

Much like Kraus, social psychologist Albert Mehrabian believes that vocalics are crucial to the reading and communication of emotion. In his book *Silent Messages*, Mehrabian proposed the 7-38-55 rule, which posits that only 7 percent of emotional meaning is carried through words, while 38 percent is carried by the volume, tone, pitch, rate, and emphasis of the voice, and the remaining 55 percent by a combination of all the other nonverbal channels (faces, gestures, postures, touch, and personal space). While other psychologists may differ on the percentages, most agree on the primary importance of vocalics in expressing our feelings.[8]

Vocalics also play a huge role in our ability to persuade, according to experiments by psychologists Alex Van Zant of Rutgers University and Johan Berger of the University of Pennsylvania, who conducted experiments in which participants were instructed to use a variety of vocalic strategies—such as modulating pitch and loudness—to persuade others to purchase a product. They found that participants who spoke fairly loudly and quickly—without hesitation—sounded more confident and were therefore much more successful at persuading others to make a purchase, even when the person doing the buying was aware that vocalic tactics were being used.[9]

VOCALICS

MAKING SURE CHILDREN learn to use and interpret vocalics appropriately from an early age is therefore an important way to ensure they will be able to effectively connect with peers later on. That's what this chapter will help you to do.

VOCALIC TYPES

In order to fully understand the nature of vocalics, it's important to understand the various types available for our use.

Volume: The volume of our voices doesn't just determine whether or not our words can literally be heard; it also impacts how we ourselves are perceived. You may remember the classic *Saturday Night Live* skit where the members of the Loud Family constantly shouted at one another, even when at a funeral, leading to all kinds of social faux pas. People who talk too loudly, even in a setting more appropriate than a funeral, are often seen as aggressive or domineering, whereas someone who talks very softly may be seen as weak or timid. And of course, when someone mutters or talks too quietly, the meaning of their words and the underlying emotion can easily be lost. Remember the *Seinfeld* episode where Kramer is dating a "low talker"? No one could understand what the poor woman was saying, but no one wanted to tell her to speak up, which created just as many social problems for her as shouting did for the Loud Family. The same is true with children: it may be endearing when a two-year-old talks too loudly or softly, but for a six-year-old such errors can hinder attempts to build peer relationships outside the home.

Pitch: The pitch of our voices can say a lot about our emotions. When we're nervous, helpless, or unsure, our voices may go up in pitch. When we're calm and confident, they may be more level. However, it's important to keep in mind that the way we read pitch in voices may be rooted in gender bias. After puberty, male voices go down in pitch and so rightly or wrongly we sometimes ascribe stereotypes based on these varying pitches—associating higher-pitched voices with weakness and youth and lower-pitched voices with strength and maturity.

Tone of voice: The exact same sequence of words can convey a wide range of meanings depending on the tone in which it is delivered. Most of us have encountered someone who speaks in a monotone, making it difficult for us to intuit how they are feeling. Those who are more expressive with their vocal tones, on the other hand, can convey a range of emotions—including excitement, sarcasm, compassion, disdain, sadness, suspicion, nervousness, to name a few—through their voice alone. Babies can pick up on vocal tones at a very young age, but they may not have the maturity to make full use of them in their own speech. Before full-time school, young children may be able to get away with speaking in a babyish tone, but as they get older, the ability to vary their tone of voice appropriately is vital in making relationships work.

Pace: Like tone, the pace of our speech can convey affective messages. We tend to talk fast when we're worked up about something—either very excited or very angry—but tend to use a slow pace when we're feeling sad or disappointed. Most adults speak at around 150 words a minute, but the pace of speech can vary from individual to individual.[10] Thankfully, as discussed, we can listen much faster than we talk, and we generally are less bothered by the fast talkers than by the slow talkers, with whom we quickly get impatient: our brains are processing the information they're imparting far faster than they are able to speak. Keep in mind that one of the best ways to connect with others is to respond to the other person's pace by varying your pace to match theirs.

Emphasis: Changing which word(s) we decide to emphasize can change the entire meaning of a sentence. To see what a difference emphasis can make, try reading the following sentences aloud.

Mary is lending me her book. (*Just Mary, not anyone else.*)

Mary **is** lending me her book. (*I insist that Mary's lending me the book.*)

Mary is **lending** me her book. (*She's not giving it, just letting me borrow it for a while.*)

Mary is lending **me** her book. (*She's not lending it to anyone else, just me.*)

Mary is lending me **her** book. (*The book belongs to Mary.*)

Mary is lending me her **book.** (*She's not lending me anything else, just her book.*)

Although these kinds of nuances may be lost on very young children, who are only just acquiring the ability to use words, if older children are unable to use or interpret emphasis accurately, it's likely to produce all kinds of confusion and misunderstandings.

Interjections: The meaningless interjections we tend to use when speaking also fall under the heading of vocalics. Interjections such as "y'know" or "like" and vocal sounds such as "um" or clearing our throat can buy us time to choose a correct word or phrase, but when interjections are overused, it can suggest we're lacking in confidence or experience or are anxious. Very young children get a free pass when it comes to interjections, but when they enter full-time school, this may be a good moment to gently correct your child when she uses "like" or "y'know" repeatedly, and to model how to speak without interjections.

> ***Other vocalics:*** Any noises that we make with our voices that *aren't* words are also considered vocalics; these include laughter, crying, screaming, gasping, tutting, sighing, coughing, and so on. Sound patterns such as "uh-uh-ah" or "hmm-humm," which tend to be used with very young children to communicate an instruction such as "don't do that," also fall into this category. Children who don't learn to control all of these many vocalic noises may be deemed disruptive by teachers and teased by peers.

Children who learn to successfully use vocalics have a significant advantage when it comes to communication and connection. Unfortunately, however, screen time has taken an especially large toll on children's ability to discriminate the emotions communicated via vocalics. Phones, tablets, and computers transmit the human voice, of course, but quality, tone, and pitch may be inferior and may not carry the same amount of information that we get from the richness and complexity of in-person speech. It takes more effort for us to communicate vocally via an audiovisual system like Zoom than it does through an audio-only medium like a phone, or in person. The greater effort saps mental energy, leading to a greater possibility of errors.

The two years we spent masked during the pandemic have also taken a toll on children's vocalics development. Masks muffle sounds, which makes it more difficult to understand not only words but also the emotions behind the words. Pasquale Bottalico, a researcher and professor in the Department of

Speech and Hearing Science at the University of Illinois, found that listeners recognized 46 percent fewer words when a speaker was masked than when unmasked. But it was *how* the words were misunderstood that has implications for emotional expression. Specifically, masks made consonants more difficult to understand—and because consonants are higher-pitched than vowels, this made it more difficult to pick up on modulations in pitch, an important cue for identifying emotions.[11] Masks also reduce the distinctions between sounds, especially in settings with poor acoustics or background noise like a crowded classroom full of children. My own research using the DANVA vocalics test showed that wearing masks made all emotions except fear harder to understand.[12]

We are now dealing with the massive long-range fallout of so much vocalic communication having taken place on screens and under artificial masked conditions once children went back to school; as a recent report found, today's teenagers have difficulty reading emotion in each other's tones of voice (although they seem better able to read emotions in adults).[13]

As with all other nonverbal channels, we must also factor in cultural differences. Only recently, scientists have begun to evaluate whether the vocal expression of emotion is universal or defined by our cultural background. Is a voice that sounds sad to an American heard as a sad voice in China? Psychologists Petri Laukka and Hillary Elfenbein analyzed the results of studies that measured the vocal *expression* of emotions within twenty-four different cultural groups as well as the ability to *identify* emotions vocally within forty-two different cultures.

What they found was that the vocal expression of positive emotions, such as happiness, do not seem to translate as well across cultures. What sounds happy to an American may not to someone from Vietnam and may even be interpreted as anger or fear. On the other hand, negative emotions like sadness are recognized more readily across cultural groups.[14]

Laukka and Elfenbein's findings have application to teaching within our increasingly diverse student population. Teachers need to be extra aware of the possibility of their students misreading their vocal expressions of emotion, as well as the possibility that they may be misreading the emotions in the vocalics of their students. One way that teachers can lower the probability of errors is to be sure to accompany their vocalics with more easily understood messages from the other nonverbal channels, like facial expressions.

VOCALICS IN INFANCY AND EARLY CHILDHOOD

The twin skills of using and reading emotion in vocalics are formed in infancy and continue to develop throughout early and late childhood. Research shows that during the third trimester of pregnancy, a child in utero can already respond to her mother's—but not her father's or siblings' voices—by moving or kicking, and that infants can recognize and distinguish a mother's voice from those of other adults in the first three weeks of life.[15] This is partly because, in the months after birth, infants can *hear* better than they can *see,* as their auditory system matures sooner than their visual one.[16]

Early on, most caregivers discover that they can use vocalics in the form of baby talk—what psychologists call "motherese" (because early research was completed primarily with mothers) or *infant-directed speech*—to grab the attention of their infants. In fact, there's a good reason why infants respond to these high-pitched, slower-paced, singsong voices: their auditory system is still immature, and so these sounds are easier for them to register. It's important to bear in mind, however, that although your baby will respond more readily to infant-directed speech than he will regular speech, it doesn't mean he necessarily understands the emotions being conveyed. That comes later when he learns to connect pitch and tone with behavioral outcomes like receiving a treat or being cuddled.

Infants' use and understanding of vocalics increase rapidly in the first year of life. At five months, babies begin to differentiate emotions presented in voices. By around two years of age, children begin to use their own voices to communicate emotion.[17] At around this age my son, for example, could playact "crying" to get my sympathy and also knew that when other children were crying, they needed to be comforted.

By three years of age, children are able to accurately identify emotions in brief vignettes using puppets, based on only vocal and situational cues. By age four, according to studies by child psychologists Bruce Morton and Sandra Trehub, young children depend more heavily on words to assess how others are feeling, but the use of vocalics then begins to reemerge as they get older. As part of their research, they had children between the ages of four and ten and young adults listen to sentences describing happy or sad events, such as "My grandma gave me a big gift!" or "My dog ran away from home," spoken in happy or sad tones of voice that sometimes matched the content of the sentence and sometimes differed. Four-year-old children, they found, focused exclusively on the content of the sentence to determine happiness or sadness, whereas by age six, children began to take vocalics into account when trying to discern meaning. The young adults in the study largely ignored the words and primarily relied on vocalics to judge which emotion was being communicated.[18]

There is growing evidence that infants and young children who become proficient in identifying and expressing emotions in voices early on do better with more complex vocalics later in childhood.[19] And children depend on parents and other caregivers to model vocalics — perhaps more so than any other nonverbal channel. Because there are no hard-and-fast rules around pitch, tone, and pace of speech, modeling is one of the main ways these skills can be taught.[20]

TIPS FOR HELPING YOUR VERY YOUNG CHILD WITH VOCALICS

1. Model vocalics deliberately.
It's never too early to demonstrate appropriate vocalic expression for your child. Infant-directed speech or baby talk is acceptable for infants but should really be phased out by the

time a child is a few months old. Certainly, as your child begins to use words of her own — around the age of two — it's important to speak to her in complete sentences and in a normal pitch. Throughout the early childhood years, you should be deliberate about modeling an appropriate range of pitch, tone, volume, speed, and vocal sounds for your child.

2. **Become aware of your own vocalic patterns.**

Vocalics differ from one person to the next. For instance, my wife is of Norwegian descent and my mother's side of the family is originally from Italy. As a result of these cultural differences, my wife tends to talk quite quietly without a lot of modulation, and I'm the opposite, as I tend to speak quickly with a lot of emphasis. As parents and grandparents, we have compensated for each other. If you don't have a diversity of vocalics in your extended family or friend group, you can find classes where students or teachers come from more diverse backgrounds. You might even want to consider enrolling your child in a second language class or dual-language early childhood program, as Cambridge University psychologists Quin Yow and Ellen Markman have found that preschool bilingual children were better at identifying emotion in a speaker's natural voice than their monolingual peers.[21]

3. **Teach your child about "indoor" and "outdoor" voices.**

Beginning around the age of two, children need to learn to control the volume of their voice. A time-honored way to explain to your child about where it's appropriate to use a loud voice and where she should use a soft voice is to explain "indoor" and "outdoor" voices: soft voices are to be used indoors, and loud voices are for outdoors.

4. Encourage your child not to whine or cry to get attention.

As every parent knows, a toddler will incessantly try to capture your attention, often by using a high-pitched whining or crying voice. When your child is whining, your instinct will likely be to give her the candy or the toy (or whatever it is that she wants) just to make the whining stop. But that sends the message that whining is a successful tactic. Instead, you can say, "Ask me again in your nice voice, not in your crying voice, please, then I will give it to you." You can help your child to learn the difference between a whining and non-whining voice by modeling both and asking him to copy you.

5. Have fun trying out different emotional tones while reading together.

Another way to practice vocalics with your child is by reading books together and speaking in the voices of the different book characters, reflecting how they feel. If someone has taken SpongeBob's favorite shell, how does he sound when he tells someone about it? Does Tigger sound happy or sad when he asks Roo, "Are you ready for some bouncing?" Many children's books will cover the primary emotions: happiness, sadness, anger, and fear.

6. Make jokes and be silly with your child.

Studies show that when parents laugh more, then children laugh more. The vocalics of laughter function as a kind of social glue, connecting us through shared amusement and joy. This can help with forming social connections down the line.

VOCALICS IN LATE CHILDHOOD

There is a lot going on with vocalics during late childhood. During this phase of rapid development, children can often misread vocalics, which can seriously interfere with their interactions in the classroom.

When I visited Ethan's first grade class, I found his teacher exasperated with his apparent unwillingness to follow her instructions, especially during transitions from one activity to another. Things had gotten so bad that the school asked if I could evaluate him for oppositional personality disorder. Children with the diagnosis of oppositional personality disorder refuse to follow rules and tend to do the opposite of what is being asked of them; they ignore instructions and are very resistant to any kind of intervention.

On my visit to the classroom, one of the first things I noticed was the way this overworked teacher was able to control her large class by simply using sound patterns. Her "uh-ah!" followed by a "mm, mm, mm," for example, sent the children a clear signal to stop what they were doing and put things away.

Ethan was the only student who didn't follow her instruction, even when she raised the intensity of her sound pattern. Finally, the teacher walked over to him and said sharply, "Ethan, stop your work!" Ethan promptly did so but looked bewildered and confused by the teacher's irritation. This was consistent with the behavior one would expect from a child with a diagnosis of oppositional personality disorder, but I thought I might have another explanation for Ethan's behavior—one that was much easier to fix.

I made a home visit to talk to Ethan's parents and see if I could uncover the root of his difficulties. Here, I observed that Ethan's family was what I would call a "loud" family, meaning that to get someone else's attention, members spoke loudly at one another. Subtle, soft-spoken communications, like those of Ethan's teacher, simply weren't on the menu. Ethan's problem, I realized, was not that he was oppositional, but rather that he came from a home in which he'd had no opportunities to learn the subtle sound patterns used by his teacher—and so they went unnoticed. Once the teacher became aware of this, she set up a few individual sessions with Ethan and found that he learned to pick up her vocal cues very quickly, once they were pointed out to him. After that, his behavior improved dramatically.

As we've seen, young children still tend to depend primarily on facial expressions to read emotion—both the content of words and the vocalic intonations are largely lost on them. By late childhood, this changes dramatically, so that by the time children finish elementary school, they will have reached a point where they should be able to rely on vocalics to read and send affective messages. For example: if you tell a four-year-old you're happy while your voice is filled with sadness, she will probably smile and tell you she's happy too. But when you do the same for a child at age ten, she's likely to tell you she's sorry you're feeling sad. She's made the leap to using vocalics to uncover the meaning behind the messages of others.

In late childhood, vocalics opens a new world of potential for communicating socially with peers, including the appropriate use of sarcasm to convey humor or irritation. Sarcasm relies on vocalics in that it uses intonation, emphasis, and pitch to imply a different meaning from that of the words being used. As a result, in order for sarcasm to work, children have to be at a stage of development in which vocalics have begun to take precedence over the meaning of words. On one of my recent school visits, I overheard an older child say, his voice dripping with snootiness, "Nice shirt," to a younger child, with the intent to embarrass him. But the child was at an age where words loomed larger than tone of voice and he simply smiled and said, "Thank you." In addition to being taught how to detect sarcasm, children of course need to be taught that sarcasm should never be used to hurt others' feelings.

In general, misreading and mis-expressing vocalics can seriously interfere with children's attempts to make friends. Take, for example, Teresa, a sweet, well-meaning girl who tends to misread fearful voice tones as happy ones. Without the ability to detect fear in a classmate's voice when declining to join in a game, her response might be to drag that child in over her objections. But when she does, she is likely to feel rebuffed when the other child yells at her or runs away. How does Teresa make sense of this? Like most children, she is completely unaware of her vocal mistakes—in her mind, she's only trying to engage with one of her classmates, but she feels rejected as a result.

In late childhood, some children may emphasize their speech and drone on in a monotone, while others might overemphasize, their voices going up and down like horses on a carousel. If either one is true of your child, you can demonstrate how to speak with a more balanced emphasis and encourage her to do the same.

Equally important is for children to react to the pace of others' speech. How do they modulate when others' pace doesn't match theirs? Most children have a preferred rate of speech, but they need to be aware of how it might differ from the pace of others', and to be flexible enough to speak slower or faster depending on the situation. This is called synchrony—the ability to modulate the rate of our own speech to match that of the person or people with whom we are interacting. Research has shown that when children's vocal interactions are in synchrony, the chance of a successful initiation of a relationship increases.[22] Interestingly, once a relationship has made it past the initiation phase, this becomes less important. But without synchrony when getting to know one another, relationships won't make it past the early stages.

TIPS FOR HELPING YOUR OLDER CHILD GET BETTER AT VOCALICS

1. **Avoid mixed messages.**

   Learning this nonverbal skill is an exercise in pattern recognition. Therefore, you should try to avoid confusing your child by speaking to her in a happy voice while your words and facial expressions express sadness or anger, and vice versa.

2. **Drop your own bad (vocalic) habits.**

   At this age, it's a good idea to model for your child how to speak without too many interjections (such as "like" and "y'know") so she doesn't pick up that particular vocal tic.

3. **Make recordings of your child's voice — and play them for her.**

   None of us enjoy hearing a recording of our voices, but nonetheless, this is the best way to become aware of how we sound to others. You can make this an enjoyable activity for your child by turning it into a game. Ask her to say the same silly phrase, "Mummy is smelly, and Daddy is smellier but [name of sibling] is the smelliest of all!" in her normal voice and record it using your phone. Then play it back for her and explain that she can change her voice in all kinds of ways. Ask her to say the same phrase again in a louder and softer voice, at a faster and a slower pace, with a higher and a lower pitch, with more intensity and less intensity. Record the phrase each time and then listen to the results.

4. **Ask your child to identify the emotional message behind your tone of voice.**

Say the same sentence in the previous example with different emotional tones of voice, as if you were happy, sad, fearful, angry, and so forth. See if your child can tell the difference.

5. **Demonstrate how emphasis works for your child.**

Take a simple sentence such as the one used earlier in this chapter—"Mary is lending me her book"—and say it out loud with your child, emphasizing a different word in the sentence each time. Talk about how emphasis changes the meaning of what she is saying. By getting her to emulate your emphasis, you're also teaching her about how to create synchrony with others.

6. **Play a vocalics guessing game.**

Watch a TV clip together, but have your child turn away from the screen and tell you what the people are feeling simply by listening to their voices. Then play the clip back with the faces and the body language to see if she guessed correctly. Some children may have an easier or harder time picking up emotions from vocalics depending on the age of the speaker; TV clips will give your child exposure to vocal qualities across a wide range of ages.

7. **Play "hot" and "cold."**

Hide something in the house or yard and just use your voice to communicate whether children are getting closer to it or farther away. This is a good game to play with a group of kids at a party or a playdate.

8. Avoid sarcasm when communicating with (or around) your child — but nonetheless explain its function.

Sarcasm is frequently used in adult interactions but should be used sparingly with and in front of younger children as it may be confusing for them (and even undermine your relationship) if you often say one thing and mean another. At the same time, your child may encounter sarcasm around other adults and peers, so it's important to explain how sarcasm works. Demonstrate sarcastic versus non-sarcastic messages for her while also explaining that sarcasm should never be used to hurt others' feelings.

WHEN YOUR CHILD NEEDS EXPERT INTERVENTION

If you feel as if your child is really struggling with both interpreting and communicating vocalics, it may be a good idea to get her hearing checked. Two to three out of every thousand children in the United States are diagnosed with hearing difficulties each year, and as hearing isn't tested quite as frequently as vision, your child could have a hearing problem that has not yet been detected.

If there are no issues with your child's hearing, you can try one of the several tests available to assess children's ability to pick up emotion in voices, including the DANVA tests. Clinical child psychologists and learning disability specialists have access to testing and interventions necessary for helping children improve their vocalic skills, but speech therapists have the most experience dealing with vocalic as well as other voice difficulties such as stuttering, lisping, and slurring.

• • • • • •

Now that we have covered the role that vocal sounds play in nonverbal communication, we turn to movements of the body and the part they play in the expression and reception of emotions.

Body language is the sixth of the major nonverbal channels and includes gestures, postures, and objectics (the things we wear on our bodies). In addition to carrying its own unique emotion information, body language acts to amplify or diminish whatever feelings are being conveyed by rhythm, facial expressions, personal space, touch, and vocalics. This crucial aspect of nonverbal communication is considered in the next chapter.

CHAPTER 8

Body Language

The Traffic Cop at the Intersection

I CONFESS THAT, THANKS IN LARGE PART TO MY PARENTS, I'M VERY good at both sending and receiving information via body language. My mother, who was Italian, never felt an emotion that she did not express immediately with her hands, arms, shoulders, and general posture. If foods weren't cooked to her satisfaction, for example, she would first wipe her hands on her apron and then raise them toward the ceiling, shaking them in frustration. My father was another case entirely. He was a large man who came from a Polish family where little emotion was expressed in general, and in gestures specifically. As a child, I had to learn to watch him carefully in order to read the minute gestural indications of his mood: a raised eyebrow, shoulders a bit slumped, hands tight, were the subtle signs indicating he was upset.

My experiences with these distinct and opposite styles equipped me with relationship skills that served me well not only as a child but also as an adolescent and adult. Thanks to my father, I became adept at noticing and interpreting body language cues that weren't always discernable to other children. Some of my elementary and high school teachers were not very expressive in their gestures, but focusing on their subtler movements clued me into what they were trying to communicate which in turn helped me to learn better in the classroom.

At the same time, my mother's dramatic body language taught me the importance of being gesturally expressive. Although I am grateful to my father anytime I am in a psychotherapy session with a taciturn client who doesn't say much verbally but reveals a lot through the way he's tightly holding his body or fidgeting with his fingers, my mother gets special thanks when I'm teaching in a large lecture class and need to connect with hundreds of students, even those in the back rows. I'm not always aware of how much I use body language as I walk about the lecture hall, with my arms and hands in constant motion. But afterward, when I find my arms and shoulders are sore, I know that I have been channeling my Italian mother.

In this chapter, we'll consider the human body as a marvelous instrument of social communication. The way we sit, stand, move our hands, place our arms, nod, lean our bodies, walk, and otherwise move carries all kinds of emotional information about us. And, in turn, the body language of others allows us to infer all kinds of emotional information about them. Often, gestures and posture will be accompanied by other forms of nonverbal communication that enhance our understanding of those affective messages. For example, when someone smiles, this may convey cheerfulness, but if they nod their head vigorously while doing so, it's more likely to convey joy. Conversely, when a smiling person has a stiff, rigid posture, with their body turned away, this is going to convey something different, and likely more complicated, than simple happiness.

Body language is not simple for children to learn. For one thing, the number of possible gestures available for use is vast. Think of the simple yet vital gesture for "stop," a hand held in front of us with the palm facing outward. This universal gesture can mean different things—from "Maybe back up a bit," to "Don't come anywhere near me!" and everything in between—depending on the angle of the hand and the speed at which it's thrust outward. In fact, psychologist Maurice Krout has identified more than five thousand different meaningful hand positions,[1] and anthropologist Gordon Hewes has isolated more than a thousand body postures in total.[2] Although the majority involve our hands and torsos, any part of the body has the capacity to communicate an affective message.

Psychologists who study nonverbal communication tend to classify gestures and postures in one of four categories: emblems, illustrators, regulators, and affectives. *Emblems* refer to gestures—most often with the hands—that have verbal equivalents, such as the gesture for "stop." Other examples are Churchill's famous *V* for victory, a wave goodbye, putting your hand to your ear to signify an inability to hear someone, or a thumbs-up to mean "okay." *Illustrators,* on the other hand, don't convey a distinct message, but they help make what a speaker is trying to communicate clearer. For example, an emphatic movement of hands suggests that the sender is excited to be making an important point (or in my mother's case, any point at all), whereas clenched fists are a sign that a person is angry, frustrated, or feeling defensive. While illustrators most often involve the hands, the torso or even the entire body may get involved as well, like in the case of someone bouncing up and down and punching the air while telling you he's just gotten some fantastic news. *Regulators* moderate the turn-taking, crucial to any successful social interaction, and include nodding, leaning forward or back, and hand gestures angled toward another person, signaling an invitation to speak. *Affectives,* the fourth and final type of gesture, are the emotional equivalent of emblems and carry a distinct emotional message, such as shaking a fist to show anger, shrugging shoulders to convey confusion, or putting our head in our hands to communicate sadness.[3]

In order to understand the power of gestures in our lives, you only have to picture a traffic cop standing at a busy intersection, cars coming and going in all directions, and consider how just one person wearing the correct kind of uniform is able to control the movement and direction of multiple cars and pedestrians and direct the flow of traffic using only her posture, arms, and hands. In our everyday lives, gestures and postures operate more subtly, usually outside of our awareness, yet like the traffic cop, they direct and control the flow of our interactions. And without them, our attempts to engage in the give-and-take of meaningful interaction can end up instead resembling the gridlock and confusion of a busy intersection in which traffic lights are broken.

WHY BODY LANGUAGE MATTERS

Body language stands apart from other forms of nonverbal communication in a number of other important ways. For one, it's the most difficult to fake. Even accomplished stage and screen actors will struggle to adapt their body language to different roles—that's because gesture and posture are almost as innate to us as our DNA and are simply not as easy to control as facial and vocal expression.

Another distinction of this particular nonverbal channel is that it's difficult if not impossible to turn off. Ever stand on the opposite side of the room and watch people having a conversation? Their bodies are constantly moving. Most people can't even sit still when talking on their phone. Their hands and arms and sometimes their legs and head position change constantly, as though the person they were talking to was right in front of them. Whether we're conscious of it or not, every movement we make sends out social and emotional information—even when we're sitting still, we're saying something through our posture.

Further, our brains process social and emotional information coming from body language faster than with any other nonverbal channel. In one fascinating study, when Hanneke Meeren and his colleagues at Tilburg University in Holland showed participants photos in which the emotion on the person's face contradicted the emotion expressed through body language (such as a smiling person standing with a dejected posture), both the verbal report of the participants and the measures of their electrical brain activity clearly showed that when the two nonverbal channels sent conflicting messages, the emotion communicated by the body won out over the facial expression. The researchers concluded that this was because the brain receives and processes social emotional information from the body faster than it does information received from the face.[4] What this tells us is that being skilled at reading gestures can give us a distinct advantage in assessing how others are feeling. If, for example, someone is greeting you with her shoulders raised toward her ears and clenched fists at her sides, you might correctly infer she's in a rage, even if she's grinning and telling you verbally that she's excited to see you.

The way we walk also communicates information about how we feel. When we step into a room with our shoulders back and head held high, this immediately projects a sense of confidence and poise to those around us — and when we project confidence, others view us more positively. Conversely, when we walk into a room with our shoulders slumped, our neck curved forward, and our chin and eyes cast down, those around us may well assume we're not having the best of days or, worse, that we don't want to be there.

Despite the advantage that correctly interpreting body language offers us, we tend to spend a surprising amount of time paying attention to what faces and voices are communicating. Psychologists Marianne Gullberg and Kenneth Holmqvist found that during our interactions we spend more than 90 percent of the time looking at others' faces, leaving only a small percentage of our attention for other sources of nonverbal information from the rest of the body.[5] Yet there are many instances in which we are forced to rely on body language because the other nonverbal channels are blocked or compromised. When someone is standing at a distance from us, for example, we must use gestures and posture to evaluate her affective state; we can't see her facial expression or hear her tone of voice. As adults, we do this instinctively at social events when deciding whether or not to approach someone—if his or her body language is open and friendly, we approach and introduce ourselves, but if the body language tells us that the person is closed off or in a bad mood, we may steer clear. During the pandemic, when most schools imposed strict social distancing rules, gestures and postures were often children's major source of emotional information. With students spaced at least six feet apart from one another, making it even more difficult to read the faces and voices that were already masked, distorted by screens, or otherwise compromised, body language became the most dependable way to communicate nonverbally, for teachers and students alike.

Gestures, Gait and Posture

The ability to adapt our body language to different situations plays a major role in our social success throughout our lives. I can still picture Ricardo, a nine-year-old child at an elementary school where I was observing various classes, whose use of expressive gestures helped make him a popular leader. When it came time to pick a captain of the school soccer team, Ricardo was the obvious choice. If the team was doing well, he would run around them with infectious enthusiasm, cheering and waving his arms, giving thumbs-up signs to the spectators, slapping the other players on the back, or high-fiving them. When the team was losing, he could lift everyone's spirits with an exaggerated shrug that seemed to say, "You did your best!" or arms raised above his head in a "Come on!" gesture to get everyone pumped up again. Despite his skill as a player, I doubt Ricardo would have been picked for this leadership role if he hadn't been equally skilled at using this nonverbal vocabulary to unite and inspire his team.

Research also shows that people who use hand gestures with fluency and frequency are more compelling and engaging in their communication and connect more easily with others. In Amy Cuddy's popular 2012 TED talk, "Your Body Language May Shape Who You Are," the social psychologist asserts that two minutes of "power posing" to loosen you up before a job interview can increase your chances of impressing the interviewer and getting hired.[6] And speaking of TED talks, a recent evaluation of TED presenters by author Vanessa Van Edwards revealed that the most popular TED talkers used close to twice as many hand gestures during their talks as the least popular one. The *type* of gestures one used also had a big impact. Popular presenters were more likely to use seven specific kinds of gestures, including one in which hands are held about eighteen inches apart as though the speaker were trying to demonstrate the size of some invisible object (known as "measure the loaf") and one where the thumb (rather than the forefinger, which is associated with scolding) is raised to emphasize an important point (known as the "fist point").[7]

Allan Pease of Macquarie University, one of the highest-rated and most viewed TED talk speakers, suggests one of the possible reasons hand gestures can make such an impact is that there are more brain connections to the human hand than to any other area of the human body.[8] Perhaps the take-home message for children who are forever fidgeting is not necessarily that they fidget less, but that they learn to use their tendencies toward expressive hand gestures to their advantage.

Our posture and gait can also have a very real impact on how we are perceived. For example, people whose arms, legs, and torsos are engaged in fluid motion when they walk are generally perceived as more confident than those who walk haltingly or stiffly. In fact, research by psychologists Brittany Blaskovits and Craig Bennell discovered that people whose strides were longer or shorter than typical, who tended to shift their weight when they walked, who only activated a part of the body or tended to move only one side of the body at a time, and who lifted their feet slightly higher than typical were more likely to fall victim to bullying or even assault.[9] Blaskovits and Bennell also pointed out that individuals who are prone to engage in bullying seemed to be especially adept at recognizing these cues of vulnerability in the walking styles of others.

The good news is that how we walk and present ourselves is learned. The child who is carrying himself in ways that invite bullying, for example, can be taught to stand up taller and prouder as a way to avoid being targeted as a victim. If you didn't grow up in or near an urban area, you may remember receiving this advice when visiting a big city for the first time: to avoid becoming a target for crime, walk rapidly, keeping your eyes down, and avoid eye contact. A friend's teenage daughter was given this very advice before going to New York City for a summer internship; she followed it and stayed safe throughout her trip. This is just one of many ways we can educate our children about how to use body language to their advantage.

Even though mastery of this particular nonverbal channel can have major social and academic benefits, most parents, educators, and caregivers don't spend much time thinking about the ways we use our bodies to communicate. Although some adults might know something about "power posing" at work, few are well versed in the importance of body language at home and in the classroom. And while parents who use more expressive body language tend to have children who use more expressive body language—as was the case with my mother and me—most parents don't give children very much guidance in this area.

For this nonverbal channel in particular, awareness can go a long way. Again, there's a classic *Seinfeld* episode to illustrate my point. "The Wink" begins with Jerry eating breakfast with Elaine and George at a restaurant. As Jerry digs into his grapefruit, he accidentally squirts juice into George's eye, causing him to blink with irritation. After breakfast, George goes to work, but unbeknownst to him, his eye is still blinking occasionally. Later that morning while George is at his desk, the president of the company comes by to ask how George is getting along with his new supervisor. George assures the president that everything is just fine, adding that he enjoys working with the supervisor—then he blinks. The president, who of course knows nothing of the earlier grapefruit incident, interprets this involuntary gesture as a wink meaning the opposite of what he is saying with his words and asks if George is having a problem with him to which George says "He's doing a great job." And blinks again! To which the president says, "I understand!" Those unintentional blinks negated George's words and twisted the entire meaning of what George was trying to convey. This happens several times throughout the rest of the episode, and by the end of the day, everyone who has interacted with George is upset with him—but he doesn't know why.

Like George, children who don't understand how to read or express body language may not realize why they are alienating others—especially if no one will fill them in about their mistakes. Imagine a child who constantly wrings his hands without realizing that the other children interpret this as anger, when really that child is just feeling nervous. Without an adult to step in and correct his mistake, he may continue to struggle socially for no good reason.

As with all the other nonverbal channels, it's important to recognize the role played by cultural differences. As Desmond Morris, an internationally recognized expert on gestures, points out, many gestures are culturally specific and so we must be particularly careful when using them in cultures different from our own. Some positive gestures in our American culture—like the popular "OK" sign, "thumbs-up" and *V* for victory or peace—are obscene ones elsewhere.[10] Roger Axtell, author of *Essential Do's and Taboos*, has written extensively about the mistakes American business travelers can make by assuming their gestures mean the same thing all over the world. One particularly embarrassing example is that of George W. Bush during the inaugural parade in 2005, when he raised his hand in the "hook 'em horns" salute—fist raised upright, index finger and pinky sticking up—to salute the University of Texas marching band as they passed by. When the photo was published worldwide, our president found out he had inadvertently angered or offended those living in Italy, where the gesture means "your wife is cheating on you," in Norway, where people thought he was saluting Satan, and in parts of Africa, where some were convinced he was issuing a curse. This cautionary tale is another reminder of the cultural complexity of nonverbal language.[11]

Objectics

Objectics are the clothes, accessories, scents, and other items that we put on our bodies to convey information about who we are. While not body language per se, they are in many ways an extension of our bodies and another nonverbal way of expressing how we feel and what we care about to the outside world. As adults, we make decisions about what to put on our bodies based not only on what we want to communicate about ourselves but also on the accepted social norms for any given situation or setting. Most people understand that how we dress for a day in the office isn't appropriate for a formal event like a wedding or gala, and that a day at the office will demand a very different outfit from one we might wear to run errands or go to the gym. Similarly, we shower, brush our hair and teeth, and keep our clothing clean in order to present ourselves in a way that is acceptable to others. As adults, we model these norms for our children and help them make appropriate choices, while trying to respect their need for self-expression.

Despite our own attention to our outward appearance, many parents will tell their children that "it's what's inside that truly counts." Such statements are well-meaning, but they ignore the reality for most school-age children, who, just like adults, have a set of unwritten rules and norms they must follow in order to be accepted by their peers. And while official dress codes are less prevalent today than when I was growing up, unofficial dress codes still very much exist, and violating them is as alienating for children as it always has been.

Young children are surprisingly attuned to what certain clothing says about them and their peers, and it's crucial for parents to understand the role that clothing plays in their lives. Starting as early as preschool, it's a way of making emotional connections and signaling that they belong to a certain group. This can be a fairly complex business, as the landscape is constantly changing. What a certain "look" says about a child when they are in first grade may mean something very different in second grade. Moreover, kids are constantly moving in and out of new friend groups and trying on new identities — and the clothes that go along with them. As parents, it's important to understand this exploration as a healthy part of growing up.

It's also important for adults to understand the degree to which the "wrong" kind of shirt or cap or insignia or hairstyle can torpedo a child's attempt to connect with others. To a parent, the difference between one T-shirt and another may feel insignificant, but other students are reading finely tuned messages in these choices — messages that adults may fail to understand or notice.

I remember one third grader I worked with, Mateo, who was having trouble making friends at school. One day, he came home crying and told his parents that other kids were teasing him about his T-shirts, which often featured flowers, teddy bears, and balloons. His parents thought these shirts were cute, fun, and innocuous, but to the kids in Mateo's class, they seemed babyish. After Mateo's announcement, his parents could have taken the "it's not the clothing that matters, it's what's inside that counts," approach, but they understood Mateo's need to fit in. They let Mateo choose his own T-shirts, and after that, he was much happier at school.

And so yes, you should let your child know that he is valuable and loved no matter what he wears, but you can still give him the tools he needs to make intentional choices. This means helping him understand how to project an image that's not only age-appropriate, but also sends the desired message about who he is and where he sees himself within his larger peer group. Some children may be okay marching to the beat of their own drum and wearing very different clothing from their peers, and that's fine too, if that is your child's intention. But for a child who *wants* to fit in and is struggling, it's worth being sensitive to your child's need to be accepted by others.

There are many ways to guide and support your child when it comes to objectics—although you may need to spend time learning about the world he inhabits and the ways that children in that world are dressing (which may be very different from the way you dressed when you were younger), then take cues from him about what would help him feel at home in it, whether that's a certain type of clothing, sparkly hair accessories, colorful elastic bracelets, or whatever other outward signifiers happen to be in favor.

Of course, these things will take on much greater importance once children enter their early teen years, but early elementary school is when they can begin to understand how social information is conveyed through clothing and other objects. Developing this understanding early forms a strong foundation for the nonverbal skills they will need to express themselves authentically, make friends, and fit in with their peers in adolescence and beyond.

BODY LANGUAGE IN INFANCY AND EARLY CHILDHOOD

Research shows that body language plays a key role in children's development. During the first few months of life, infants have little control over the muscles necessary for many adult gestures. Although they may thrash their arms and legs around, perhaps in great joy or great annoyance, such flailing doesn't really carry much meaning. However, at around nine months, they have enough command of their movements that they can begin to use basic gestures such as pointing, which is typically one of the first gestures to appear. But by the end of their first year, they will have learned several additional gestures, including waving, shaking head, putting hands over eyes (to play peekaboo), poking, grabbing or pulling, reaching for something they want, showing you something or giving you something, as well as clapping. At this age, these gestures all carry a similar meaning: a request for your attention.

These early attempts at communication set the stage for infants' development of verbal and social language, functioning as a first language of sorts. In fact, body language constitutes the nonverbal channel most closely tied to verbal language acquisition because the area of the brain used for processing gestures is the same area that will be used when words enter the picture. Months before a baby utters the word "No!" she will be able to vigorously shake her head from side to side to communicate the same message. Once she's learned the gesture for "No!," it's then a small step to make the sound "Nah!" before firmly closing her mouth as she shakes her head from side to side to let you know that she doesn't want to eat her oatmeal, leaving a trail of mush all over her face and possibly you, too. Before you get upset with your child, it's worth remembering that gestural ability at this age has been found to predict verbal language ability some two years later, which in turn predicts later academic success.

Like most new parents, you've likely marveled at your child's ability to effectively communicate in this way at such a young age. Parents and other caregivers are usually delighted when infants wave hello or blow kisses goodbye, but in truth, these gestures are more than an adorable party trick. By greeting and saying farewell to others, your child is beginning to participate in the give-and-take necessary for social interactions. Throughout early childhood, your child will use gestures to gain attention and form social bonds. I treasure memories of the way my little grandson would raise his arm straight over his head for me to grasp when taking his first steps with the sure expectation that I would be there to help him maintain balance. What may seem to have been a simple gesture to prevent himself from falling was also an important social transaction: his way of confirming expectations of emotional as well as physical support. In this case, his gesture invited the comfort of touch, as it often does during the first two years of life.

By sixteen months children will have refined their earlier gestures and added nodding as well as some culturally specific gestures, like high fives, to their repertoire. Sixteen months is a significant developmental milestone; research shows that they should have learned at least sixteen gestures at this point. (See the following sidebar for more on these milestones.)

Posture also plays a key role in a child's body language at this young age.[12] As Michael Tomasello, an internationally recognized researcher in developmental psychology, has shown, the connection between posture and action is present from as early as two years old. Tomasello and his colleagues have used posture as the basic way to measure children's satisfaction with their actions. For example, they found that two-year-old children showed an "elevated" posture—the infant equivalent of an adult standing straight and tall—after achieving a goal or helping another achieve a similar goal, even without a reward. In other words, children begin to express their feelings—in this case, pride—through their bodies in the same way adults do from toddlerhood on.[13]

GESTURE MILESTONES IN VERY EARLY CHILDHOOD

By twelve months

Waving: At first, you may not be sure whether your baby is intentionally waving or simply flailing arms, but with time, encouragement, and practice, waving becomes well-defined and associated with saying hello and goodbye.

Shaking the head: This universal gesture of refusal usually arrives before the affirmative nod for "yes." For most children, this is the first gesture that offers them some sense of power and control over their lives.

Putting hands over eyes: This gesture, necessary for playing peekaboo, is associated with another developmental milestone, known as object permanence: the ability to understand that a person or object hasn't disappeared even when they can't see it.

Grabbing or pulling on you: This is an infant's way of getting your attention.

Reaching: This gesture can be a way of asking to be given something (usually by wiggling a hand back and forth), to be picked up, or to be moved in the direction of a desired person or object.

Showing and giving: An infant may attempt to engage you in an interaction of some kind by bringing you a toy or another object. This may be a request to play or a request for help; either way, "showing and giving" is the precursor to the more complex ways of initiating a social interaction that your child will learn in the years ahead.

Pointing: Perhaps the most important of all gestures in early childhood, pointing is an infant's way of participating in the uniquely human interaction called "joint attention." It can also be a crucial component of verbal language development, as when an infant points to an object, then turns to the caregiver to make eye contact, after which the caregiver says the word for the object being pointed at. If an infant is routinely slow to respond (or is nonresponsive) to a caregiver's attempts to direct their attention by pointing toward a person or object, it may be (though is not necessarily) an early indication of developmental delay sometimes associated with autism.

Clapping: This gesture may come as early as six months or as late as nine. It's used to indicate general excitement, to entertain, or as an invitation to engage in give-and-take.

Blowing a kiss: One of the most endearing gestures, blowing a kiss is performed with others to get attention, engage, and express affection.

Putting an index finger over the lips: The universal "shhh" gesture indicates the need for quiet (though if and when this gesture emerges depends on whether and how often it is used by the adults in the infant's life).

By sixteen months
(note that these gestures carry a specific meaning, rather than reflecting general desires)

Nodding: At sixteen months your child should be able to communicate both "yes" and "no" using body gestures.

Waving a hand up and down in front of the nose: By the age of sixteen months, children should be able to use this gesture to indicate "stinky."

Putting a hand up with the palm facing out: The sixteen-month-old child should be able to use this gesture to communicate "stop" or "wait."

> **Other symbolic gestures:** By sixteen months of age, children should be able to use gestures such as thumbs-up, or shrugging to say "don't know."

TIPS TO HELP YOUR CHILD WITH BODY LANGUAGE IN EARLY CHILDHOOD

1. Play and interact with your child using gestures.

For generations, parents have played simple games with their children such as peekaboo and patty-cake. Such joyful actions are, in fact, important business. During the first eighteen months of life, children are learning to use gestures and signs to communicate their desires, needs, and preferences by observing the gestures used by those around them. In these earliest stages of childhood, it's a good idea to think of this type of play as providing infants with a vocabulary that will continue to grow in complexity as time goes on. You can take your child's hands and move them together to replicate clapping or waving or blowing kisses. Then show him how to perform these gestures by demonstrating them yourself. Repetition is crucial. Gestures aren't learned in one try but rather become absorbed by performing the same movements again and again over many weeks.

2. Introduce turn-taking early on.

When you catch your child making a movement such as waving his hands in excitement, you can wave your hands excitedly in response. Copy your child and wait for him to make another movement, then copy that one. By taking turns communicating via gestures, you are teaching him the give-and-take that is at the core of successful social interactions.

3. **Initiate pointing early on, using your voice and smiling face to encourage your child.**

   First, point at something — for example, a cup — then smile and say with a happy voice, "Cup!" Repeat this often. Again, learning language — both verbal and nonverbal — takes time and repetition.

4. **Carefully select TV shows that will help children learn about gestures.**

   Remember that the American Academy of Pediatrics recommends no screen time for infants under eighteen months, except for video chats with relatives, and then after eighteen months, limited screen time with parents or caregivers there to supervise. However, after about eighteen months you can find TV shows that will help children to better understand gestures, such as the loveable robot WALL-E and Scrat the *Ice Age* squirrel, who don't need words to communicate how they feel.

5. **Let your child lead through gestures.**

   When you are interacting with your child, wait for him to use invitational gestures such as pointing, showing, or reaching to let you know what he would like to do together. Too often, adults want to direct a child's play, but when you let a child lead, you are allowing him not only to choose but also to communicate that choice with you.

6. **Don't be afraid to use big, exaggerated gestures and movements to engage your child.**

Think about the way that sports mascots keep children entertained by waving their hands, pointing this way and that, doing little dances. This is how they are able to connect with and keep children's attention—all without saying a single word.

7. **Enroll your young child in classes and activities that involve movement and gesture, such as Music Together classes (described in chapter 3), dance classes, or martial arts.**

Taking some kind of movement class will help your child build coordination and other physical skills that are so useful in learning to express themselves nonverbally using their bodies.

BODY LANGUAGE IN LATE CHILDHOOD

I'll never forget sitting in an auditorium at a school where I was consulting and overhearing the two first graders next to me as they tried to make sense of a routine being performed up onstage by two visiting mime artists. To me, it was clear that they were miming getting ready for school in the morning, but my two young friends were confused. The first one said, "This is so funny... they're having trouble milking a cow!" "No," the other one said loudly, "they're getting their rocket together to blast off to the moon!" Listening to their speculation reminded me that without context, young children struggle to identify gestures and their meaning.

In late childhood, children need to have access to a whole range of gestural skills. It's during this phase that they will be attempting to engage their peers in relationships independently of their parents, which will require them to identify turn-taking cues and other nonverbal messages conveyed via hands and postures. Think about the negative effect it would have on the beginning of a relationship if the child walked toward another child but didn't understand the meaning of the gesture for "stop" and continued to invade that child's personal space despite her outstretched hand.

Depending on what they have learned at home, school can be a place where weaknesses can be turned into strengths. But too often, children who are having difficulties in this area will have no idea that their body language is the source of their social troubles—and neither will the adults around them. This was the case with Charlotte, an eight-year-old girl I was asked to evaluate, who was having more than her share of disagreements with her peers. Observing her in the classroom, I couldn't see anything problematic about her behavior. She paid attention to the teacher and worked diligently on her school assignments. Her teacher told me she was doing well in all her subjects, especially English, and that she was polite and well-behaved. However, when I went to observe her during recess on the playground, I saw a quite different Charlotte.

At this age, children's body language on the playground tends to split along gender lines. The boys will usually form groups of three or more, jostling among themselves and talking to one another while standing side by side. In contrast, the girls tend to pair off, keeping a close but respectful distance from each other, facing each other while talking, and using their hands to express excitement and enthusiasm. But Charlotte stood apart from her classmates with her arms folded tightly across her chest. Based on her posture, she looked less like a child and more like an older woman, an effect that was reinforced when she unfolded her arms to point at other children as though she was scolding them. Needless to say, her body language wasn't going over well with her peers, who were turning their backs on her, shaking their heads, and keeping their distance, all nonverbal indicators of failed connection.

Charlotte, it turned out, had a very off-putting "resting posture." Similar to the "resting face," the resting posture is the one we automatically and unconsciously assume when we are in neutral gear. However, just as with resting faces, children's resting posture can communicate a negative emotion even if they aren't actually feeling that way. When children see a fellow student walking around with a lowered head and slouched body, they are likely to assume the child is unfriendly, aloof, or stuck-up. Meanwhile, teachers may assume that the child is unhappy or even surly, when that may not be the case.

When the source of Charlotte's problems was explained to her parents and teachers, they scheduled times to talk with her to help her become aware of what her body language was saying to others. That's when they learned that Charlotte was often mimicking her favorite aunt, who was a schoolteacher, and that the two of them often spent time playing school together—hence the very adultlike and sometimes stern-looking posture. After this was discovered, I asked if Charlotte's aunt could be enlisted to explain to Charlotte that although schoolteachers can stand apart from children and instruct them from a distance, young children are supposed to play and interact with one another. It didn't take long for Charlotte's use of gestures, and in turn her friendships, to improve.

Unless corrected, however, young children with negative resting postures may carry this error with them into adulthood. I remember seeing a young man at the request of his manager at a large corporation. The employee in question was bright, polite, pleasant, and motivated, but as I soon discovered, his resting posture involved sitting back in his tilted chair, with his legs spread outward, sometimes with one of them draped over another chair, behavior that was both off-putting to his workmates and smacked of unprofessionalism. Teaching children about the importance of gesture and posture at a young age can help prevent social and professional challenges like this one later in life.

TIPS FOR HELPING YOUR OLDER CHILD WITH BODY LANGUAGE

1. **Take time to review basic gestures with your child.**

   By four years old, he should be able to understand what gestures are and how they are used to begin an interaction. Review universal gestures with him, such as the "shhh" sign, stop sign, thumbs-up, high five. Make sure he understands what these basic gestures mean — it's easy to assume children will have picked this up, but because it's rare for gestures to be taught, your child may well be in the dark. In particular, children may not be aware of the powerful message our hands can deliver. To demonstrate this, you can show him the distinction between the hand movement that communicates "stop" in a gentle way (with hand slightly lowered) and the hand movement that sends a more emphatic "STOP" (hand extended with the palm perpendicular), then practice these gestures together.

2. **Take your child to some noisy place, like a mall, where spoken language can't be heard properly, and have him observe how people are interacting with one another.**

   Ask him to pick out gestures that he sees around him and identify ones he knows and doesn't know. Have him take a guess at what's going on between people based on their gestures, by asking "What do you think those two people are talking about?" You can also ask him what he thinks about a person, just from watching their body language from a distance. Ask your child who looks friendly or whom he would like to meet and why. You can even turn it into a game by having your child craft a story about a stranger, based on what your child imagines that person is like.

3. **Have your child practice standing with different levels of confidence.**

   Talk to your child about posture and standing up straight, and what to do with his hands while standing. Observe whether your child is standing with his hands in his pockets, fidgeting, or flailing. Then ask him to stand like the teacher, or various classmates, and see if he can differentiate between and imitate these postures.

4. **Practice a variety of postures with your child and ask him how he feels when doing each.**

   See if he can communicate the four basic emotions—happiness, sadness, anger, and fear—using his body. Ask him to notice how the different postures make him feel on the inside and explain that while he may be sitting that way because he's sad, sitting that way can also *make* him feel sad—and that a happy, confident posture, on the other hand, can help him feel happier and more confident.

5. **Embrace fidgeting.**

   As your child becomes older, your instinct may be to tell him to always sit still, hands folded, bottom on seat, in situations where you want him to pay attention. But research suggests that sitting rigidly in one place creates a greater "cognitive load" on children, taking energy away from what they should be learning, and that kids should be allowed to fidget and move their bodies, whether to express themselves or to just let off steam. Many schools now allow children to fidget in their chairs, modifying classrooms to include a variety of different areas where students can stand while being instructed, or where they can be more energetic or engage in sensory play. This is why fidget toys are often embraced in classrooms, because they satisfy a child's need to be in motion while still focusing on the lesson.

6. **When watching television, mute the sound and see if your child can guess how people are feeling just by focusing on their gestures.**

Since your child will also be able to see faces, have him try to connect faces with gestures. Do the gestures always correspond to what facial expressions are communicating?

7. **Watch sports together.**

Sports are a gold mine for teaching body language, since players need to be constantly communicating with each other nonverbally, often across long distances, like a baseball diamond or soccer field. American football, for example, is filled with gestures of all kinds, from hand signals indicating a first down to tacklers pumping fists in the air after a good play or clasping hands to forehead after a bad one. Shows like *So You Think You Can Dance* and *Dancing with the Stars* are also good sources of gestural learning. Talk to your child about the ways that the performers and athletes are communicating using their bodies.

8. Play charades with your child.

This game almost seems to have been invented to teach the use of gestures. You can play basic charades, or you can make it more challenging by asking everyone to wear a mask. Without access to facial expressions, contestants will have to rely on posture, gesture, and body language clues alone.

9. Take your child to age-appropriate theater performances.

Onstage, actors will often use exaggerated body language to communicate emotions to the audience, making this a great way for children to learn about the meanings behind various gestures. On the way home, talk about how the actors used their bodies to portray their characters. Ask your child if he noticed the way the actors said "thank you" at the end by bowing, and how the audience communicated their appreciation by clapping or giving a standing ovation.

10. Enroll your child in theater, improv, or mime classes.

These will inevitably teach how to use gestures and body language to communicate.

11. Model appropriate self-presentation.

Remember that the objectics a child puts on his body are also a form of nonverbal communication. Talk to your child about appropriate ways to dress, depending on the occasion, while modeling appropriate choices yourself. And make sure he understands the importance of basic hygiene and grooming.

WHEN YOUR CHILD NEEDS EXPERT INTERVENTION

Although most children will modify their gestures and postures once they are made aware of them, some children may take longer to adapt and adjust. Enlisting professionals who focus on movement and dance is very helpful here for longer-term remediation. Registered Dance/Movement Therapists can present a structured program for children to follow, and movement therapists can work with children to better understand what they might be missing in reading others' movements and sending their own. Acting classes can help them learn more about the power of gestures and postures to communicate feelings, not only one-on-one but to larger audiences. And yoga classes (many studios offer classes specifically for children) may also help your child become more aware of his or her own body in space. The Music Together program for preschoolers and Rhythm Kids for elementary-age children may also be helpful, as there are more than a few similarities between the roles of rhythm and gestures in the turn-taking process; in addition, gestures like clapping, pointing, and hand movement play a prominent role in music classes.

CONCLUSION

There are few things that makes a parent's heart leap for joy quite like hearing your child say, "I made a new friend." Of course you feel pleased for and proud of your child, but it's more than that. Learning that your child is liked by others will remind you of the happiness *you* experienced in childhood playing with friends or perhaps of how painful it felt to be rejected or left out of the game.

It's normal to feel sad or helpless when your child is struggling socially. After all, no parent wants their child to be unhappy, and it's all too easy to blame ourselves when we see that our child is in pain.

It's also normal to be confused about when and how to intervene. Young children aren't expected to have mastered all the nonverbal skills that we as adults often take for granted, and it's not always easy to know whether a behavior you are witnessing is a cause for concern or merely a function of your child's age. Complicating matters further, some children are simply more introverted than others, and on the surface, it's not always clear whether a child sitting alone at recess feels excluded or is perfectly content reading a book alone instead of joining in on a game. But regardless of age, personality, or individual preferences, one truth is universal: having friends and getting along with peers is central to children's present and future happiness.

I am a scientist practitioner, which means that what I recommend professionally is based as much as possible on what is known through science and research. But I also am the oldest of five siblings and worked for years on playgrounds and had the unique pleasure of coaching under-eight soccer teams. Because I am a big brother, a father, and a grandfather I know children don't always fit snugly into the theoretical and clinical boxes scientists say they should. Parenting is complicated, difficult, and not for the faint of heart. What I can say for sure is that you, as a parent, have the power to shape your child's future happiness in simple yet profound ways.

Not so long ago, I was finishing up a meeting with a younger colleague who was also the mother of two young children, ages four and six. I happened to mention I was writing a book about children the same age as hers to prepare them for a different world than the one she and I had experienced growing up. That's when she turned to me and with an anxious tone in her voice asked, "Dr. Nowicki, am I raising my children the right way?" She told me she had observed that other parents seemed to be spending their weekends driving their children around, rushing from one place to another, enrolling their kids in multiple activities or taking them on expensive outings. "But all I want to do when I have the time is to spend it with them!" she said. "Is that wrong? Is just being with them doing enough to prepare them for the future?"

Here's the answer I gave her: Yes, it's absolutely enough to prepare them for the future. When you put your phone away and spend time with your children doing the simplest of activities, like playing a board game, going to the park to throw a ball around, or taking a walk around the neighborhood, you are teaching them innumerable lessons about the language of relationships, which is nonverbal, and one of the most important things we can learn as human beings.

It's very easy to feel the pressure of keeping up with other parents so your child doesn't "miss out." So many parents I meet feel the need to get their children into the best nursery school, preschool, kindergarten, to enroll children in multiple after-school programs and camps, and to pack their kids' weekends with swim lessons and soccer games and art classes, fearful that if their sons and daughters don't begin developing these hobbies and skills early (in some cases, *very* early), they will be locked out of the best colleges and universities. Although children can certainly benefit from good schools and some carefully chosen extracurricular activities, it can be easy to overlook how much children gain from unstructured face-to-face time with family, friends, neighbors, and the wider community. The simple truth is that teaching most children to communicate nonverbally is well within the power and expertise of all parents, and children don't need to attend multiple classes and activities per week in order to learn the skills they need to succeed socially. The first step is to become aware of what nonverbal language is and why it matters, and the second step is to help your children become aware of this too. The third step is to model the kind of nonverbal language you would like your children to use and involve them in activities and experiences that will reinforce what you are teaching them. It's really that simple, and it's really that important.

Now more than ever, parents need to step up to help fill the learning gaps created by modern life, but you don't need to do it alone. Teachers, grandparents, extended family, and community members—in the form of babysitters, neighbors, coaches, and others—can also play a role. I still remember, with enormous fondness, the part that teachers in particular played in my own acquisition of nonverbal language. Thanks to them, I learned new ways of interacting with peers, many of whom behaved differently from the people I had gotten to know in my family and neighborhood. Under the guidance of these adults, I gradually became better at reading and expressing my feelings, not only using words but, more importantly, in my facial expressions, tones of voice, and body language. What I learned at school along with what I experienced at home provided me with a foundation for the skills I needed to grow and thrive, both socially and academically, in the future. I hope teachers will read this book and come away with a better understanding of the crucial role they can play in this aspect of children's development. If you are a teacher reading this: thank you. You already do so much for our children. I hope this book will help you foster even greater connections with your students.

Grandparents and other older members of the community can play an equally vital part. Recently, I had the pleasure of visiting a former colleague whose six-month-old grandchild was staying with her at the time. I knew her as an accomplished academic, but now I was seeing her for the first time as a grandparent, bouncing her baby grandson on her knee, making silly faces and noises at him, and playing patty-cake. No screens were involved, no technology was used, no passwords were needed to join; it was just a loving grandmother making faces and sounds varying in loudness and tone to make her grandson smile and giggle, holding his hands and guiding them back and forth as they clapped together. During these simple, loving interactions the child was learning about all kinds of nonverbal communication, including turn-taking, rhythm, touch, and more. As grandparents we are not always comfortable with technology, but this can turn out to be a strength because we are more likely to depend on old-fashioned face-to-face interactions when we are with our grandchildren. My own grandchildren are teenagers now, but they still remember making silly faces at our dinner table or doing a "happy dance" when they came to visit us as young children. And what remains most vivid to them was not the words we used, but the nonverbal language we "spoke" when with them. Grandparents are a hidden resource for educating one's children in the use of nonverbal language, but they are not the only family members available to help. Uncles and aunts, cousins, and others may be gifted at interacting with your children in ways you may not be, further exposing your child to the nonverbal skills needed to connect and make friends.

If you're not lucky enough to have close family living nearby — or even if you are — it's worth thinking about other ways that you can expand your child's community beyond immediate family. Children's learning can also benefit from interactions with peers and adults, especially those from all kinds of different racial and cultural backgrounds. Seek out opportunities for your child to be social with a diverse mix of people and in a diverse range of settings, through playdates, playgroups, and other age-appropriate activities that involve meeting up with peers. Take care not to overschedule your child, however: you want to be able to give her the time and space to learn at her own pace. Let the interactions evolve and don't rush your child as she learns new skills. Give her the opportunity to repeat interactions with others to establish effective patterns of communicating nonverbally.

And never forget that you already have the tools you need to ensure your child has a happier future. With that in mind, before I leave you, here are some final tips for fostering healthy nonverbal communication in your child.

CONCLUSION

DURING INFANCY

1. **The single most important thing for you to do during this phase is to spend time playing with your baby.**

Research dating back to the beginnings of the Head Start initiative in the 1960s has consistently found that infants who are spoken to, smiled at, and cuddled by their caregivers are more likely to be happy and socially adjusted in late childhood. Play provides opportunities for your baby not only to experience these nonverbal signs of affection but also to learn the give-and-take of human interaction, a complex dance choreographed by nonverbal action.

2. **Take the time to tune into your baby's emotional states.**

Psychiatrist Daniel Siegel says that we are tuned into an infant's emotional state when we align our states, our primary emotions, through the sharing of nonverbal signals.[1] To accomplish this connection—what Siegel calls "resonance"—you need to spend enough time observing your infant's facial expressions and body movements to be able to appropriately gauge feelings of frustration, fear, joy, and satisfaction.

3. **See the world from your baby's perspective.**

While it may seem a little silly, the act of seeing the world from your baby's physical perspective will help you to better understand his emotional perspective. I remember trying this out by lying down on the floor in my son's bedroom and staring up at his ceiling. It was remarkable how this point of view gave me insight into what my son was seeing on a daily basis. I nearly jumped a mile when my wife's face suddenly appeared above me, asking me why I was lying on the floor. I realized at that moment how different people's facial expressions and body movements can appear when they are looming over you.

DURING EARLY CHILDHOOD

1. Name that feeling and separate it from behavior.

Just as much as parenting can be an emotional roller coaster, your very young child has his own emotions he's dealing with. When a child misbehaves, throws a tantrum, or becomes stubbornly defiant, most of this emotion is communicated nonverbally: through facial expressions, tone of voice, and body language. As a parent, it's important to focus on the nonverbal messages that accompanying this behavior—"I see you have an angry face." Then identify the emotions they convey—"I can tell you are feeling frustrated because you're clenching your fists"—and discuss them with your child. When your child uses words to say he is angry, sad, anxious, or frightened, let him know you also can see it in his face, posture, and gesture and hear it in his voice as you offer him comfort. This helps him connect words to both feelings and nonverbal expression.

2. Caregivers don't always have to be positive: children need to know how to deal with negative feelings.

Being an active father and grandfather has shown me that sometimes the most useful interactions with children deal with negative feelings—both mine and theirs. Attempting to be upbeat and positive all the time is an unattainable goal. Moreover, it's not always helpful to your child. Just because you don't want to yell or cry in front of him doesn't mean you need to keep your emotions to yourself. We know from research that our emotions leak out through our tone, facial expressions, and body language, regardless of how much we try to hold them inside. Children will sense these emotions whether you verbalize them or not. As parents, we're all familiar with those moments when we get angry or frustrated or we snap in irritation. Once you've calmed down, try to engage with your child again. Explain that you got angry or frustrated but you've calmed down, using a warm tone of voice and a soothing rhythm, and reinforce these reassuring messages via touch. You can also take note of children's nonverbal responses to your outbursts and how they shift once you have talked it through.

3. Use the "one in five" rule.

The often-offered idea of a "one in five" rule means giving your child at least four positive affirmations per every one criticism. But there is no magic about "one in five" itself; the rule could be "one in three" or "one in seven." Simply put, instead of being too eager to lead with criticism or point out what your child did wrong, you spend far more time accentuating and paying attention to what your child did right. Researchers have found that to be happy, people need more positives than negatives in their lives. When it comes to facial expressions, you can comment positively whenever you see your child succeeding in reading and communicating via this important nonverbal channel. "I noticed you gave that girl a big smile. That must have made her feel good!" "I saw you looked right at Mom's new friend and gave her such a nice handshake. I bet it really made her feel welcome to our house." "I saw you noticed that Billy looked sad about not being included in the game and went over to talk to him. Good for you!"

DURING LATER CHILDHOOD

1. Debrief with your child about his school day.

When you ask your child about his school day, then listen to and sympathize with him as he recounts the day's events, remember to resist the urge to correct and direct as you did in early childhood. At this age, children must be given the freedom to make and learn from interpersonal mistakes in order to grow socially.

Whenever possible, you can use these casual conversations as an opportunity to reinforce nonverbal learning. Research shows that children pick their friends very quickly on the basis of nonverbal indicators, often without much reflection or awareness. Discuss the nonverbal signals that may have drawn the child to a certain peer over another: a smiling face or nod of encouragement, a confident posture or presence, a shared rhythm or manner of speaking, and so on.

2. Provide multiple contexts in which to socialize.

Late childhood is a time for your child to experience a variety of situations with a variety of different people. Each of these represents an opportunity to experience different ways of relating and expressing himself nonverbally and to pick up nuances that may not have been learned in infancy or early childhood within the family. After-school sports and activities can provide extremely useful exposure to this kind of nonverbal diversity, but it's a good idea to avoid enrolling your child in *too many* activities. This can end up being overwhelming for your child, leaving him no time to process what's been experienced. Just like adults, children have varying amounts of energy for social interaction. If your child resists these experiences because he is shy or socially anxious, you can encourage him by spending more time with people he already knows—such as cousins—before gradually introducing him to others who are less familiar to him.

ACKNOWLEDGMENTS

The irony is not lost on me that I have written 80,000 words and now want to acknowledge individuals who have helped to show that words may not be as important as we thought.

To be certain, this book could not have been written without the foundational theorizing of Harry Stack Sullivan and the early research efforts of Paul Ekman, Irenaus Eibl-Eibesfeldt, Ray Birdwhistell, Robert Rosenthal, and Judith Hall, among others, whose work legitimized the scientific study of nonverbal phenomena. I offer special thanks to Daniel Goleman, whose book *Emotional IQ* first brought the importance of nonverbal behavior and skill into public awareness.

As I look back to see how I got to this place and to writing this book I am reminded once more of the significance of relationships in my life.

I begin with my parents and my relationship with them. Though both were supportive of me throughout my childhood, they related to me in very different ways. My mother spoke often using a mix of English and Italian words that made it difficult at times for me to comprehend exactly what she was trying to communicate. In contrast, my father rarely spoke at all. So as a child and later as an adolescent and adult I learned to pay attention to their other communications, tones of voice, gestures, postures, facial expressions, and the like to understand how they felt and where I stood with them.

I am in debt to my present family as well. My wife, Kaaren, son Andy and his wife, Jenny, Jenny's brother, Jason, and my two grandchildren, Hannah Ruth and Soren. They have provided me love and support as well as making me aware that there are countless ways to read and express emotions nonverbally over time and situations. I learned so much from watching my grandchildren's rudimentary skill in nonverbal communication grow with each passing year. But it was Kaaren who provided the stability and support when I needed it most. When I needed honest and useful criticism or loving support, it was to her and her alone that I have always turned.

My first formal learning experience in nonverbal communication took place during my clinical psychology internship at Duke University Medical Center. My clinical supervisors Robert C. Carson and Derek Shows introduced me to the theorizing and clinical work of Harry Stack Sullivan, whose thinking centered on relationships and the significance of nonverbal communication in their growth or decline. My training with Carson and Shows made me sensitive to what I and my clients were communicating in psychotherapy with our gestures, tones of voice, and facial expressions. I took this insight with me when I left my internship and accepted my first, and what turned out to be my only, academic position at Emory University. It was there I met Marshall P Duke, and it was through my relationship with him that my ideas about nonverbal communication truly grew and blossomed.

ACKNOWLEDGMENTS

My partnership with Marshall led to research papers and books in which we expanded our thoughts about why some relationships grew and flowered while others wilted and died. We constructed reliable and valid ways of measuring nonverbal behavior and wrote about the role of nonverbal communication in everyday interactions and in psychotherapy. During this time, we were fortunate to have input from another Emory colleague, Donald J. Kiesler, a renowned psychotherapy researcher, who had worked with Carl Rogers, the founder of client-centered therapy. Along with our academic experiences, our work as consultants to public and private schools allowed us to see more clearly how nonverbal communication played a part in students' academic success and social adjustment. Public exposure through appearances on television shows like Oprah Winfrey and CBS *Good Morning* were instrumental in bringing our early work to the attention of the general public. I cannot overestimate what my relationship with Marshall has meant in my life. I may be the author of this book, but his presence is to be found everywhere in it.

Then there are the relationships I've had with my students, both graduate and undergraduate. I can't imagine my academic and personal life without them. The basic tests developed to assess nonverbal skills, the Diagnostic Analysis of Nonverbal Accuracy (DANVA) and the Emory Dyssemia Index (EDI), resulted from my partnerships with students: John Carton (Adult and child faces), Alexandra Rothman, nee Demertzis (child paralanguage), Kym Baum (adult paralanguage), Hallee Pitterman, nee Altman (adult postures). Elizabeth Bromley was responsible for the development of the nonverbal observational

ACKNOWLEDGMENTS

rating scale called the Emory Dyssemia Index. As testimony to the worth of their efforts, the tests have been successfully used in hundreds of studies that have increased our knowledge of how nonverbal communication functions in relationships.

Many of my doctoral students made the commitment to make nonverbal communication the focus of their dissertations: Rachel Ammirati, Wendy Bailey, John Carton, Marietta Collins, Eileen Cooley, Denise Glanville, Mark Hartigan, Lisa Heiman, Jeff Jones, Tom Kay, Cindy Lancelot, Lauren Maxim, Erin McClure, Laura Mufson, John Paddock, Amy van Buren, Karen Schwartz, and Virginia Wickline. I can't thank them enough for their efforts and contributions.

Colleagues also joined me in publishing articles and chapters on nonverbal communication, especially Nancy Bliwise, Kristin Byron, William Gentry, and Ann Van Buskirk. Each in their own way helped me to gain new insights about how nonverbal communication operated in our lives.

I am especially thankful for the contributions to my thinking and writing of Meryl Lipton, founder and past director of the Rush Neurobehavioral Center. We published a major theoretical paper describing a structure for the study of nonverbal communication in neurodivergent as well as neurotypical children, and we found we shared a dedication to helping children realize their full potential. It was indeed fortunate that when our paths crossed, we had the good sense to join one another and continue our clinical research travels together on the same road.

Sara Salmon is executive director of the Center for Safe Schools. A fierce advocate for children's safety and education, her annual meetings in Denver were an opportunity for me to meet and learn from public and private school teachers and administrators in a way I could not anywhere else.

Next, I have to "travel" overseas to acknowledge a truly special relationship with an amazing individual, Jean Golding. I met Jean when I gave an invited talk at Bristol University in England nearly four decades ago, and we have been research partners and close friends ever since. She is responsible for launching and maintaining a truly monumental longitudinal study of children and their parents that began in 1994 and is still going strong today. I was allowed to administer the DANVA to both parents and children when the children turned eight, and it resulted in a unique set of data that has enabled researchers to study the parent child relationship in ways they couldn't have before.

None of what I wanted to write would have made it to the pages of this book if it were not for Bridget Mazie, my agent. Some dozen years ago Emory sponsored a day-long program to help faculty learn about how to develop ideas into books. I attended panel discussions in the morning, where agents and editors described what it took to get a book published. I was fortunate enough to snag a fifteen-minute individual session with Bridget in the afternoon. Thin-slice research studies suggest that you only need a brief time to make accurate judgments about others based on their nonverbal behavior. Fifteen minutes was more than enough time for me to decide I wanted Bridget to be my agent. Thank heaven she agreed. Since that time Bridget has given birth to three children and helped me publish two books. I'm not sure which of these two was the more difficult task for her to complete.

ACKNOWLEDGMENTS

I must give an extra thank you to Bridget for introducing me to Justin Brouckaert. Justin helped to shape my ideas and guide me to write a clear, cogent proposal, without which this book would not have been possible.

And then there is Eve Claxton. I've given much thought to how best to describe our time together, and here's what I've come up with. When Edmond Hillary became the first to climb Mount Everest he was celebrated around the world for his accomplishment. But Hillary would never have made it to the top if it were not for sherpa Tenzing Norgay who guided and supported him all the way to the summit. Eve was my sherpa, keeping me on track and providing support when I needed it most. I can't thank her enough. As if that weren't enough, during one of our Zoom meetings she introduced me to her adorable four-year-old niece, Gloria. On this occasion, Gloria, dressed as a fairy princess, waved the wand she was carrying and pronounced to Eve and me that the book was going to be a success. Talk about important relationships!

With all this help you wouldn't think I'd be fortunate enough to find a relationship that tops them all, but you'd be wrong. My experience with my editor, Talia Krohn, has been life-changing. There has not been a moment in our relationship when she did not have my back. She has been kind, instructive, and supportive. From fearing what she might think of what I wrote, I became eager to read her feedback. Talia always had my back and never wavered in guiding me in the right direction to write the book I wanted to write. In short, Talia made writing RASSC the most profoundly satisfying academic experience of my life.

NOTES

Introduction

1. Harry Stack Sullivan, *Conceptions of Modern Psychiatry* (New York: W. W. Norton, 1953).

2. Stephen Nowicki and Marshall P. Duke, *Helping the Child Who Doesn't Fit In* (Atlanta: Peachtree Publishers, 1992).

3. Daniel Goleman, *Emotional Intelligence* (New York: Bantam Books, 1995).

4. Jean Twenge, "Have Smartphones Destroyed a Generation?" *Atlantic*, September 15, 2017, https://www.theatlantic.com/magazine/archive/2017/09/has-the-smartphone-destroyed-a-generation/534198/.

5. *Richard Weissbourd et al.*, "National Survey of Loneliness—Loneliness in America: How the Pandemic Has Deepened an Epidemic of Loneliness and What to Do About It," Making Caring Common, Harvard Graduate School of Education, President and Fellows of Harvard College, February 9, 2021, https://mcc.gse.harvard.edu/reports/loneliness-in-america.

6. National Survey of Children's Health, 2021, Child and Adolescent Health Measurement Initiative (CAHMI), Data Resource Center for Child and Adolescent Health.

7. Samantha Brooks et al., "The Psychological Impact of Quarantine and How to Reduce It," *Lancet* 395, no. 10227 (February 26, 2020): 912–920, https://doi.org/10.1016/S0940-6736(20)30460-8.

8. Joan Hope, "Research Shows Impact of COVID-19 on Students with Disabilities, Other Groups," *Disability Compliance for Higher Education* 27, no. 6 (2021): 9, https://doi.org/10.1002/dhe.31205.

9. Nicole Racine et al., "Global Prevalence of Depressive and Anxiety Symptoms in Children and Adolescents during COVID-19: A Meta-analysis,"

NOTES

JAMA Pediatrics 175, no. 11 (August 9, 2021): 1142–1150, https://doi.org/10.1001/jamapediatrics.2021.2482.

10. "Covid 19 Pandemic Triggers 25% Increase in Prevalence of Anxiety and Depression Worldwide," World Health Organization, March 2, 2022, https://www.who.int/news/item/02-03-2022-covid-19-pandemic-triggers-25-increase-in-prevalence-of-anxiety-and-depression-worldwide.

11. Yan Liu et al., "Associations between Feelings/Behaviors during COVID-19 Pandemic Lockdown and Depression/Anxiety after Lockdown in a Sample of Chinese Children and Adolescents," *Journal of Affective Disorders* 284 (February 5, 2021): 98–103, https://doi.org/10.1016/j.jad.2021.02.001.

12. Hope, "Research Shows Impact of COVID-19."

13. Evie Blad, Educators see gaps in kids' emotional growth due to the pandemic. Education Week February 24, 2022.

14. Social emotional learning: 10 trends in 10 charts. Results of a national survey. EdWeek Research Center. November, 2022.

15. Twenge, "Have Smart Phones Destroyed a Generation?"

16. Věra Skalická, et al., "Screen Time and the Development of Emotion Understanding from Age 4 to Age 8: A Community Study," *British Journal of Developmental Psychology* 37, no. 3 (February 28, 2019): 427–443, https://doi.org/10.1111/bjdp.12283.

17. Yalda T. Uhls et al., "Five Days at an Outdoor Education Camp without Screens Improves Preteen Skills with Nonverbal Emotion Cues," *Computers in Human Behavior* 39 (October 2019): 387–392, https://doi.org/10.1016/j.chb.2014.05.036.

Chapter 1

1. Stephen Nowicki and Marshall P. Duke, *Helping the Child Who Doesn't Fit In* (Atlanta: Peachtree Publishers, 1992).

2. Sarah Z. Cole and Jason S. Lanham, "Failure to Thrive: An Update," *American Family Physician* 83, no. 7 (2011): 829–834.

3. Julianne Holt-Lunstad, "Social Connection as a Public Health Issue: The Evidence and a Systemic Framework for Prioritizing the 'Social' in Social Determinants of Health," *Annual Review of Public Health* (2022): 193–213, https://doi.org/10.1146/annurev-publhealth-052020-110732.

4. Kathleen B. King and Harry T. Reis, "Marriage and Long-Term

Survival after Coronary Artery Bypass Grafting," *Health Psychology* 31, no. 1 (2012): 55–62, https://doi.org/10.1037/a0025061.

5. Barry M. Lester et al., *Resilience in Children* (Hoboken, NJ: Wiley-Blackwell, 2006).

6. Harry S. Sullivan, *Conceptions of Modern Psychiatry*, 2nd ed. (W. W. Norton, 1966).

7. Melissa Faye Greene, The Left-Out Child, *Family Life*, September, 1993, page 104.

8. Sigmund Freud, *The Problem of Anxiety* (New York: W. W. Norton, 1936).

9. Sullivan, *Conceptions*.

10. Morten L. Kringelbach et al., "On Cuteness: Unlocking the Parental Brain and Beyond," *Trends in Cognitive Sciences* 20, no. 7 (2016): 545–558, https://doi.org/10.1016/j.tics.2016.05.003.

11. Edward Tronick et al., "Infant Emotions in Normal and Pertubated Interactions," in *Biennial Meeting of the Society for Research in Child Development*, Denver, CO (1975).

12. Albert Mehrabian, *Silent Messages: Implicit Communication of Emotions and Attitudes*, 2nd ed. (Belmont, CA: Wadsworth, 1980).

13. M. D. S. Ainsworth et al., *Patterns of Attachment* (Hillsdale, NJ: Erlbaum, 1978).

14. M. P. Duke and S. Nowicki, "A Social Learning Theory Analysis of Interactional Theory Concepts and a Multi-dimensional Model of Human Interaction Constellations," in *Handbook of Interpersonal Psychotherapy*, ed. J. C. Anchin and D. J. Kiesler (Elmsford, NY: Pergamon, 1982), 78–94; Stephen Nowicki and Marshall P. Duke, *Will I Ever Fit In?* (Atlanta: Peachtree Publishing, 2012); S. Nowicki and A. van Buskirk, "Non-verbal Communication: From Good Endings to Better Beginnings," in *Nonverbal Communication in Close Relationships: What Words Don't Tell Us*, ed. R. Sternberg and A. Kostić (London: Palgrave Macmillan, 2022), 277–305.

Chapter 2

1. Marco Bani et al., "Behind the Mask: Emotion Recognition in Healthcare Students," *Medical Science Educator* 31, no. 4 (2021): 1273–1277, https://doi.org/10.1007/s40670-021-01317-8.

2. Daphne J. Holt et al., "Personal Space Increases during the COVID-19 Pandemic in Response to Real and Virtual Humans," *Frontiers in Psychology* 13 (2022): 952–998, https://doi.org/10.3389/fpsyg.2022.952998.

NOTES

3. Alison Prato, "Does Body Language Help a TED Talk Go Viral?" *TEDBlog,* May 12, 2015, https://blog.ted.com/body-language-survey-points-to-5-nonverbal-features-that-make-ted-talks-take-off/.

4. Amy J. C. Cuddy et al., "Preparatory Power Posing Affects Nonverbal Presence and Job Interview Performance," *Journal of Applied Psychology* 100, no. 4 (2015): 1286–1295, https://doi.org/10.1037/a0038543.

5. Ray L. Birdwhistell, *Kinesics and Context*, London: Allen Lane, The Penguin Press, 1971.

6. Mario Pei, *The Story of Language* (Philadelphia and New York: J. B. Lippincott Company, 1949).

7. David G. Weissman et al., "Low Emotional Awareness as a Transdiagnostic Underlying Psychopathology in Adolescence," *Clinical Psychology Science* 8 (2020): 1-18.

8. Paul Watzlawick et al., *Pragmatics of Human Communication: A Study of Interactional Patterns, Pathologies and Paradoxes*, (New York: W. W. Norton & Co., 2011).

Chapter 3

1. J. Margraf et al., "Social Rhythm and Mental Health: A Cross-Cultural Comparison," *PLOS One* 11, no. 3 (2016): 1–17.

2. Alexis Wnuk, "This Is Why You Get Zoom Fatigue," BrainFacts, September 23, 2020.

3. Koen de Reus et al., "Rhythm in Dyadic Interactions," *Philosophical Transactions of the Royal Society B* (2021), https://doi.org/10.1098/rstb.2020.0337.

4. M. Dolsen, J. Wyatt, and A. Harvey, "Sleep, Circadian Rhythms, and Risk across Health Domains in Adolescents with an Evening Circadian Preference," *Journal of Clinical Child and Adolescent Psychology* 48, no. 3 (2019): 480–490.

5. C. J. Zampella et al., "Interactional Synchrony and Its Association with Social and Communication Ability in Children with and without Autism Spectrum Disorder," *Journal of Autism and Developmental Disorders* 50, no. 9 (2020): 3195–3206, https://doi.org/10.1007/s10803-020-04412-8, PMID: 32065341, PMCID: PMC7569722.

6. Ken Fujiwara, Masanori Kimura, and Ikuo Daibo, "Rhythmic Features of Movement Synchrony for Bonding Individuals in Dyadic Interaction," *Journal of Nonverbal Behavior* 44 (2020): 273–293.

7. Noboru Kobayashi, The Soothing Effect of the Mother's Heart Beat, Child Research Net. 2003.

NOTES

8. G. Markova, T. Nguyen, and S. Hoehl, "Neurobehavioral Interpersonal Synchrony in Early Development: The Role of Interactional Rhythms," *Frontiers in Psychology* 10 (2019): 2078.

9. David Deming, "Early Childhood Intervention and Life-Cycle Skill Development: Evidence from Head Start," *American Economic Journal: Applied Economics* 1, no. 3 (2009): 111–134, https://doi.org/10.1257/app.1.3.111.

10. K. Guilmartin and L. M. Levinowitz, *Music and Your Child: A Guide for Parents and Caregivers* (Princeton, NJ: Music Together, 1992); K. Guilmartin and L. M. Levinowitz, *Teaching Music Together* (Princeton, NJ: Music Together, 2003).

11. T. C. Rabinowitch and A. Knafo-Noam, "Synchronous Rhythmic Interaction Enhances Children's Perceived Similarity and Closeness toward Each Other," *PLOS One* 10, no. 4 (2015): e0120878, https://doi.org/10.1371/journal.pone.0120878.

12. William J. Friedman, "Development of Time Concepts in Children," *Advances in Child Development and Behavior* 12 (1978): 267–298, https://doi.org/10.1016/S0065-2407(08)60040-3.

13. Fangbing Qu et al., "Development of Young Children's Time Perception: Effect of Age and Emotional Localization," *Frontiers in Psychology* (2021), https://doi.org/10.3389/fpsyg.2021.688165.

14. Sandra Stojic, Vanja Topic, and Zoltan Nadasdy, "Children and Adults Rely on Different Heuristics for Estimation of Durations," *Scientific Reports* 13 (2023).

15. T. Berny et al., "Construction of a Biological Rhythm Assessment Scale for Children," *Trends in Psychiatry and Psychotherapy* 40, no. 1 (2018), https://doi.org/10.1590/2237-6089-2017-0081.

Chapter 4

1. Morten L. Kringelbach et al., "On Cuteness: Unlocking the Parental Brain and Beyond," *Trends in Cognitive Science* 20, no. 7 (2016): 545–558, https://doi.org/10.1016/j.tics.2016.05.003.

2. Jordon Lite, "Kids' Smiles Predict Their Future Marriage Success: Childhood Photos Reveal Happiness Levels Later in Married Life," *Scientific American*, September 1, 2009, https://www.scientificamerican.com/article/kids-smiles-predict-their-future/.

3. LeeAnne Harker and Dacher Keltner, "Expressions of Positive

NOTES

Emotion in Women's College Yearbook Pictures and Their Relationship to Personality and Life Outcomes Across Adulthood," *Journal of Personality and Social Psychology* 80, no. 1 (2001): 112–124, https://doi.org/10.1037/0022-3514.80.1.112.

4. Eric Savitz, "The Untapped Power of Smiling," *Forbes Daily Newsletter*, March 22, 2011, https://www.forbes.com/sites/ericsavitz/2011/03/22/the-untapped-power-of-smiling/?sh=410f68b97a67.

5. Claus-Christian Carbon and Martin Serrano, "The Impact of Face Masks on the Emotional Reading Abilities of Children—a Lesson from a Joint School–University Project," *i-Perception* 12, no. 4 (2021): 1–17, https://doi.org/10.1177/20416695211038265.

6. Marco Bani et al., "Behind the Mask: Emotion Recognition in Healthcare Students," *Medical Science Education* 31, no. 4 (2021): 1273–1277, https://doi.org/10.1007/s40670-021-01317-8.

7. Jennifer M. B. Fugate and Courtny L. Franco, "Implications for Emotion: Using Anatomically Based Facial Coding to Compare Emoji Faces across Platforms," *Frontiers in Psychology* 12 (2021), https://doi.org/10.3389/fpsyg.2021.605928.

8. Jonas Aspelin, "Enhancing Pre-service Teachers' Socio-emotional Competence," *International Journal of Emotional Education* 11, no. 1 (2019): 153–168, https://www.frontiersin.org/articles/10.3389/fpsyg.2021.605928/full.

9. Judy Foreman, "A Conversation with: Paul Ekman; The 43 Facial Muscles That Reveal Even the Most Fleeting Emotions," *New York Times*, August 5, 2003, https://www.nytimes.com/2003/08/05/health/conversation-with-paul-ekman-43-facial-muscles-that-reveal-even-most-fleeting.html.

10. Albert Mehrabian, *Silent Messages: Implicit Communication of Emotions and Attitudes*, 2nd ed. (Belmont, CA: Wadsworth, 1980).

11. Pamela M. Cole and Amber E. Jacobs, "From Children's Expressive Control to Emotion Regulation: Looking Back, Looking Ahead," *European Journal of Developmental Psychology* 15, no. 6 (2018): 658–677, https://doi.org/10.1080/17405629.2018.1438888.

12. Elisabet Serrat et al., "Identifying Emotional Expressions: Children's Reasoning About Pretend Emotions of Sadness and Anger," *Frontiers in Psychology* 11 (2020): 1–10, https://doi.org/10.3389/fpsyg.2020.602385.

13. Charles Darwin, *The Expression of Emotions in Man and Animals* (New York: Oxford University Press, 1872).

NOTES

14. Rachael E. Jack et al., "Facial Expressions of Emotion Are Not Culturally Universal," *Psychological and Cognitive Sciences* 109, no. 19 (2012): 7241–7244, https://doi.org/10.1073/pnas.1200155109.

15. David Matsumoto, *The SAGE Handbook of Nonverbal Communication* (Thousand Oaks, CA: SAGE Publications, 2006), 219–235, https://doi.org/10.4135/9781412976152.

16. Rachael E. Jack, Roberto Caldara, and Philippe G. Schyns, "Internal Representations Reveal Cultural Diversity in Expectations of Facial Expressions of Emotion," *Journal of Experimental Psychology: General* 141, no. 1 (2012): 19–25, https://doi-org/10.1037/a0023463.

17. Denise N. Glanville and Steve Nowicki Jr., "Facial Expression Recognition and Social Competence among African American Elementary School Children: An Examination of Ethnic Differences," *Journal of Black Psychology* 28, no. 4 (2002): 318–329, https://doi.org/10.1177/009579802237540.

18. Amy G. Halberstadt et al., "Preservice Teachers' Racialized Emotion Recognition, Anger Bias, and Hostility Attributions," *Contemporary Educational Psychology* 54 (2018): 125–138, https://doi.org/10.1016/j.cedpsych.2018.06.004.

19. Eleanor J. Gibson and Richard D. Walk, "The 'Visual Cliff,'" *Scientific American* 202, no. 4 (1960): 64–71, https://doi.org/10.1038/scientificamerican0460-64.

20. Amy Halberstadt, Susan Denham, and Julie Dunsmore, "Affective Social Competence," *Social Development* 10, no. 1 (2001): 79–119.

21. Malinda, Carpenter, and Michael Tomasello. Joint attention and imitative learning in children, chimpanzees and enculturated chimpanzees Social Development no.4 (1995): 1299-1311.

22. Ludy T. Benjamin and Darryl Bruce, "From Bottle Fed Chimp to Bottlenose Dolphin: A Contemporary Appraisal of Winthrop Kellogg," *The Psychological Record* 32, 1982.

23. Tiffany Field and Tedra Walden, "Production and Discrimination of Facial Expression by Preschool Children," *Child Development* 53, no. 5 (1982): 1299–1311, https://doi.org/10.2307/1129020.

24. Megan E. Harrison et al., "Systematic Review of the Effects of Family Meal Frequency on Psychosocial Outcomes," *Canadian Family Physician*, 61 no. 2 (2015): 96-106.

25. Reginal B. Adams, A. J. Nelson, and Devin Purring, "Eye Behavior," in *Nonverbal Communication,* ed. Judith A. Hall and Mark L. Knapp (Berlin/

Boston: Walter de Gruyter, 2013, 233–261; Jodi Schulz, "Eye Contact: Don't Make These Mistakes," Michigan State University, Michigan State University Extension, December 31, 2012, https://www.canr.msu.edu/news/eye_contact_dont_make_these_mistakes.

26. Hironori Akechi et al., "Attention to Eye Contact in the West and East: Autonomic Responses and Evaluative Ratings," *PLOS One* 8, no. 3 (2013): e59312, https://doi.org/10.1371/journal.pone.0059312.

Chapter 5

1. Michael Graziano, *The Spaces between Us* (New York: Oxford University Press, 2018).

2. Edward T. Hall, *The Hidden Dimension* (New York: Doubleday, 1966).

3. Agnieszka Sorokowska et al., "Preferred Interpersonal Distances: A Global Comparison," *Journal of Cross-Cultural Psychology* 48, no. 4 (2017), https://doi.org/10.1177/00220221176980309.

4. Marshall Duke and Stephen Nowicki Jr., "A New Measure and Social Learning Model for Interpersonal Distance," *Journal of Experimental Research in Personality* 6 (1972): 1–17.

5. Duke and Nowicki, "A New Measure."

6. Graziano, *Spaces between Us*.

7. Graziano, *Spaces between Us*, 158–159.

8. Daphne J. Holt et al., "Personal Space Increases during the COVID-19 Pandemic in Response to Real and Virtual Humans," *Frontiers in Psychology* 13 (2022), https://doi.org/10.3389/fpsyg.2022.952998.

9. Thomas M. Horner, "Two Methods of Studying Stranger Reactivity in Infants: A Review," *Journal of Child Psychology and Psychiatry* (1980), https://doi.org/10.1111/j.1469-7610.1980.tb01796.

10. Giulia Orioli et al., "Identifying Peripersonal Space Boundaries in Newborns," *Scientific Reports* 9 (2019), http://doi.org/10.1038/s42598-019-45084-4.

11. Yair Bar-Haim et al., "Attachment in Infancy and Personal Space Regulation in Early Adolescence," *Human Development* 4, no. 1 (2002): 68–83. http://doi.org/10.1080/14616730210123111.

12. Duke and Nowicki, "A New Measure"; F. N. Willis, R. Carlson, and D. Reeves, "The Development of Personal Space in Primary School Children,"

Journal of Nonverbal Behavior 3 (1979): 195–204, https://doi.org/10.1007/BF01127363.

Chapter 6

1. Eric Fishman et al., "Touch Relieves Stress and Pain," *Journal of Behavioral Medicine* 18 (1995): 69–79, https://doi.org/10.1007/BF01857706.

2. Pavel Goldstein et al., "The Role of Touch in Regulating Inter-Partner Physiological Coupling during Empathy for Pain," *Scientific Reports* 7, no. 1 (2017), https://doi.org/10.1038/s41598-017-03627-7.

3. Sheldon Cohen et al., "Does Hugging Provide Stress-Buffering Social Support? A Study of Susceptibility to Upper Respiratory Infection and Illness," *Psychological Science* 26, no. 2 (2014): 135–147, https://doi.org/10.1177%2F0956797614559284.

4. Carissa J. Cascio et al., "Social Touch and Human Development," *Developmental Cognitive Neuroscience* 35 (2019): 5–11, https://doi.org/10.1016/j.dcn.2018.04.009.

5. Cascio et al., "Social Touch," 6.

6. April H. Crusco and Christopher G. Wetzel, "The Midas Touch: The Effects of Interpersonal Touch on Restaurant Tipping," *Personality and Social Psychology Bulletin* 10, no. 4 (1984): 512–517, https://doi.org/10.1177/0146167284104003.

7. Aino Saarinen et al., "Social Touch Experience in Different Contexts: A Review," *Neuroscience and Behavioral Reviews* (2021): 360–372, https://doi.org/10.1016/j.neubiorev.2021.09.027.

8. Harry F. Harlow et al., "Total Social Isolation in Monkeys," *Proceedings of the National Academy of Sciences of the United States of America* 54, no. 1 (1965): 90–97, https://doi.org/10.1073%2Fpnas.54.1.90.

9. Juulia T. Suvilehto et al., "Topography of Social Touching Depends on Emotional Bonds between Humans," *Psychological and Cognitive Sciences* 112, no. 45 (2015): 13811–13816, https://doi.org/10.1073/pnas.1519231112.

10. Disa Bergnehr and Asta Cekaite, "Adult-Initiated Touch and Its Functions at a Swedish Preschool: Controlling, Affectionate, Assisting and Educative Haptic Contact," *International Journal of Early Years Education* 26, no. 3 (2017): 312–333, https://doi.org/10.1080/09669760.2017.1414690.

11. Laura Crucianelli, "The Need to Touch," *Aeon*, April 12, 2020, https://aeon.co/essays/touch-is-a-language-we-cannot-afford-to-forget.

NOTES

12. David J. Linden, *Touch: The Science of the Hand, Heart, and Mind* (London: Viking, 2015).

13. Cascio et al., "Social Touch."

14. Francis McGlone et al., "Discriminative and Affective Touch: Sensing and Feeling," *Neuron* 82, no. 4 (2014): 737–755, https://doi.org/10.1016/j.neuron.2014.05.001.

15. Charles A. Nelson et al., *Romania's Abandoned Children: Deprivation, Brain Deprivation, and the Struggle for Recovery* (Cambridge, MA: Harvard University Press, 2014), 416.

16. Nelson et al., *Romania's Abandoned Children*.

17. Pamela M. Owen and Jonathan Gillentine, "Please Touch the Children: Appropriate Touch in the Primary Classroom," *Early Child Development and Care* 181, no. 6 (2011): 857–868, https://doi.org/10.1080/03004430.2010.497207.

Chapter 7

1. Michael Kraus, "Voice-Only Communication Enhances Empathic Accuracy," *American Psychologist* 72, no. 7 (2017): 644–654.

2. Leonor Neves et al., "Associations between Vocal Emotion and Socio-emotional Adjustment in Children," *Royal Society Open Science* 8 (2021): https://doi.org/10.1098/rsos.211412.

3. Alexia D. Rothman and Stephen Nowicki, "A Measure of the Ability to Identify Emotion in Children's Tone of Voice," *Journal of Nonverbal Behavior* 28, no. 2 (2004): 67–92, https://doi.org/10.1023/B:JONB.0000023653.13943.31.

4. Bruce J. Morton and Sandra E. Trehub, "Children's Understanding of Emotion in Speech," *Child Development* 72, no. 3 (2001): 834–843.

5. Rebecca Lake, "Listening Statistics: 23 Facts You Need to Hear," CreditDonkey, September 17, 2015.

6. Lake, "Listening Statistics."

7. Simon Leipold et al., "Neural Decoding of Emotional Prosody in Voice-Sensitive Auditory Cortex Predicts Social Communication Abilities in Children," *Cerebral Cortex* (2022): 1–20.

8. Albert Mehrabian, *Silent Messages: Implicit Communication of Emotions and Attitudes* (Belmont, CA: Wadsworth, 1971).

9. Alex B. Van Zant and Jonah Berger, "How the Voice Persuades,"

NOTES

Journal of Personality and Social Psychology (2019), http://dx.doi.org/10.1037/pspi0000193.

10. Lake, "Listening Statistics."

11. Pasquale Bottalico et al., "Effect of Masks on Speech Intelligibility in Auralized Classrooms," *Journal of the Acoustical Society of America* 148 (2020): 2878–2884, https://doi.org/10.1121/10.0002450.

12. Marco Bani et al., "Behind the Mask: Emotion Recognition in Healthcare Students," Medical Science Educator 31, no. 4 (2021): 1273–1277, https://doi.org/10.1007/s40670-021-01317-8.

13. Michele Morningstar, Joseph Venticinque, and Eric C. Nelson, "Differences in Adult and Adolescent Listeners' Ratings of Valence and Arousal in Emotional Prosody," *Cognition and Emotion* 33, no. 7 (2019): 1497–1504.

14. Petri Laukka and Hillary Anger Elfenbein, "Cross-Cultural Emotion Recognition and In-Group Advantage in Vocal Expression: A Meta-analysis," *Emotion Review: Emotion in Voice* 13, no. 1 (2021): 3–11.

15. Tawni B. Stoop et al., "I Know That Voice! Mothers' Voices Influence Children's Perceptions of Emotional Intensity," *Journal of Experimental Child Psychology* 199 (2020): 1–20.

16. Marie-Helene Grosbras, Paddy D. Ross, and Pascal Belin, "Categorical Emotion Recognition from Voice Improves during Childhood and Adolescence," *Scientific Reports* 8 (2018).

17. Carlos Hernandez Blasi et al., "Voices as Cues to Children's Need for Caregiving," *Human Nature* 33 (2022): 22–42.

18. J. Bruce Morton and Sandra E. Trehub, "Children's Understanding of Emotion in Speech," *Child Development* 72, no. 3 (2001): 834–843.

19. Neves et al., "Associations between Vocal Emotion."

20. Carolyn Quam and Daniel Swingley, "Development in Children's Interpretation of Pitch Cues in Emotion," *Child Development* 83, no. 1 (2012).

21. W. Quin Yow and Ellen M. Markman, "Bilingualism and Children's Use of Paralinguistic Cues to Interpret Emotion in Speech," *Bilingualism: Language and Cognition* 14, no. 4 (2012): 562–569, https://doi.org/10.1017/S1366728910000404.

22. Koen de Reus et al., "Rhythm in Dyadic Interactions," Philosophical Transactions of the Royal Society B 376, no. 1835 (2021), https://doi.org/10.1098/rstb.2020.0337.

NOTES

Chapter 8

1. Maurice Krout, "Further Studies on the Relation of Personality and Gesture. A Nosological Analysis of Autistic Gestures," *Journal of Experimental Psychology* 20, no. 3 (1937): 279–287.

2. Gordon W. Hewes, "The Anthropology of Posture," *Scientific American*, February 1, 1957, https://www.scientificamerican.com/article/the-anthropology-of-posture/.

3. Peter Bull and John P. Doody, "Gesture and Body Movement," in *Nonverbal Communication*, ed. Judith Hall and Mark Knapp (Berlin/Boston: De Gruyter, 2013).

4. Hanneke K. M. Meeren et al., "Rapid Perceptual Integration of Facial Expression and Emotional Body Language," *Proceedings of the National Academy of Sciences of the United States of America* 102, no. 45 (2005): 16518–16523, https://doi.org/10.1073%2Fpnas.0507650102.

5. Marianne Gullberg and Kenneth Holmqvist, "What Speakers Do and What Listeners Look At: Visual Attention to Gestures in Human Interaction Live and on Video," *Pragmatics and Cognition* 14, no. 1 (2006): 53–82, https://doi.org/10.1075/pc.14.1.05gul.

6. Amy J. C. Cuddy et al., "Preparatory Power Posing Affects Nonverbal Presence and Job Interview Performance," *Journal of Applied Psychology* 100, no. 4 (2015): 1286–1295, https://doi.org/10.1037/a0038543.

7. Alison Prato and Vanessa Van Edwards, "Does Body Language Help a TED Talk Go Viral? 5 Nonverbal Patterns from Blockbuster Talks," *TEDBlog*, May 12, 2015, https://blog.ted.com/2015/05/12/body-language-survey-points-to-5-nonverbal-features-that-make-ted-talks-take-off.

8. Allan Pease, "The Power Is in the Palm of Your Hands" (presentation at Macquarie University, Sydney, Australia, February 11, 2014).

9. Brittany Blaskovits and Craig Bennell, "Are We Revealing Hidden Aspects of Our Personality When We Walk?" *Journal of Nonverbal Behavior* 43 (2019): 329–356, https://doi.org/10.1007/s10919-019-00302-5.

10. Desmond Morris, *Peoplewatching: The Desmond Morris Guide to Body Language* (London: Jonathan Cape, 2002).

11. Roger E. Axtell, *Essential Do's and Taboos: The Complete Guide to International Business and Leisure Travel* (Hoboken, NJ: John Wiley & Sons, 2007).

12. BabySparks, "Baby Gestures: An Important Language Skill,"

Speech, BabySparks, February 16, 2018, https://babysparks.com/2018/02/16/baby-gestures-an-important-language-skill/.

13 Robert Hepach, Amrisha Vaish, and Michael Tomasello. The Fullfillment of Others' Needs Elevates Childen's Body Posture. Developmental Psychology, 53, no. 1 (2017): 100-113. http://dx.doi.org/10.1037dev0000173.

Conclusion

1. Daniel Siegel and Mary Hartzell, *Parenting from the Inside Out: How a Deeper Self-Understanding Can Help You Raise Children Who Thrive* (New York: Tarcher/Penguin, 2004).

INDEX

NUMBERS
7-38-55 rule, 176

acceptance, 43
accessories, 207
acting classes, 225
affect bursts, 175
affective touch, 157
affectives, 197–198
age. *see* early childhood; infancy and infants; late childhood
American Academy of Pediatrics, 79, 216
American culture
    expressions, intensity of, 105
    gestures in, 206
    greetings, 56
    space bubbles in, 126
    time, concept of, 85
Angelou, Maya, 73
anger, 97, 110
anxiety, 10–12
Asian culture
    eye contact in, 117
    time, concept of, 85
assault, 204
attachment relationship, 35
audience, connecting with, 63–64
autism, 214
awareness
    instilling sense of rhythm

    in early childhood, 77
    in late childhood, 88–89
    lack of, 57–58
    of racial bias, 106

baby talk, 36–37, 183, 184
beat, mimicking, 79
Bennell, Craig, 203–204
Berger, Johan, 176
Bergnehr, Disa, 154
bias, 105–106
Biological Rhythm Interview of Assessment in Neuropsychiatry for Kids (BRIAN-K), 91
Birdwhistell, Ray, 54
birth, 34–36
Black Americans, 105
Blaskovits, Brittany, 203–204
blowing kiss, 214
body language, 195–225
    emotional messages transmitted by, 33
    importance of, 199–210
        gestures, gait and posture, 202–207
        objectics, 207–210
    in infancy and early childhood
        gesture milestones in, 213–215
        overview, 210–212
        tips for helping, 215–217
    in late childhood
        overview, 217–220
        tips for helping, 221–225

257

INDEX

body language *(cont.)*
  overview, 51–52
  when expert intervention is needed, 225
body parts, 162–163, 167
Bottalico, Pasquale, 180–181
bowing, 56
BRIAN-K (Biological Rhythm Interview of Assessment in Neuropsychiatry for Kids), 91
Brooks, Samantha, 10–11
bullying, 204

Carbon, Claus-Christian, 96
Cascio, Carissa, 149
Cekaite, Asta, 154
charades, 224
child gulags, 158
Chinese culture
  expressions, intensity of, 105
  eye contact in, 117
choice phase, relationship, 41–42
"chums" (friendships), 39–40, 138. *see also* relationships
clapping, 214
clothes, 207–210
cognitive load, 222–223
Comfortable Interpersonal Distance (CID) scale, 128
complexity, of communication, 54
conduct disorder, 10
"consensual validation," 40
consent, 50, 141
criticism, 235–236
Crucianelli, Laura, 155
Crusco, April, 149
crying voice, 186
C-touch fibers, 148–149, 157, 166
Cuddy, Amy, 202
culture
  etiquette around touch in, 152
  expressions, intensity of, 105–106
  eye contact and, 117

language shaped by, 56–57
time, concept of, 85
using gestures in different, 206–207
vocal expression of emotions, 181–182
cyberspace, 131

dance therapists, 225
dancing, 88
  helping with body language, 217
  instilling sense of rhythm, 78–79
Dancing with the Stars, 223
DANVA (Diagnostic Analysis of Nonverbal Accuracy) test, 96–97, 120, 174, 194
darting, 116
Darwin, Charles, 104
death, relationships and, 28–33
deepening phase, relationship, 43–44, 137–138
depression, 10–12
developmental disabilities, 3–4
Diagnostic Analysis of Nonverbal Accuracy (DANVA) test, 96–97, 120, 174, 194
discriminatory touch, 157
dress codes, 208
dual-language early childhood program, 185
Duchenne, Guillaume-Benjamin-Amand, 104
"Duchenne smile," 104
Duke, Marshall, 41, 97
dyspraxia, 129
dyssemias, 27

early childhood
  body language in
    gesture milestones in, 213–215
    overview, 210–212
    tips for helping, 215–217
  facial expressions in
    overview, 106–109
    tips for helping, 110–113

INDEX

fostering healthy nonverbal communication during, 234–236
how nonverbal language develops in, 36–38
personal space in
  overview, 132–134
  tips for making visible and concrete in, 134–136
physical touch in
  overview, 157–159
  tips for introducing to, 159–163
rhythm in
  Head Start program, 76–77
  tips to help instill, 77–79
vocalics in
  overview, 182–184
  tips for helping, 184–187
"Education in a Pandemic" (Hope), 11
EdWeek Research Center, 13
Ekman, Paul, 104
Elephant and Piggie books (Willems), 112
elevators, space inside, 142
Elfenbein, Hillary, 181–182
emblems, 197–198. *see also* gestures
emojis, 99
emoticons, 99
Emotional Intelligence (Goleman), 6
emotional messages
  accepting nonverbal, 60–61
  affectives, 198
  expressed by body language, 33
  identifying with tone of voice, 192
  scope of emotional cues, 54
  using emoticons and emojis, 99
  wearing masks and recognizing, 97
emotions
  associated with touch, 157
  concealing, 103
  displayed in picture books, 111–112
  infants reading, 109
  muscles in face producing, 102
  role relationships play in development of, 29
  wearing masks and recognizing, 180–181
empathy, 76
emphasis, 179, 192
English language, 54
European culture, space bubbles in, 126
exaggeration
  helping with body language, 217
  rhythm with, 74
expert intervention
  for body language, 225
  for facial expressions help, 120
  for help with physical touch, 168
  for personal space preferences, 142
  for rhythm help, 90–91
  for vocalics, 193–194
The Expression of Emotions in Man and Animals (Darwin), 104
expressive language skills, 55–56
extracurricular activities, 228–229, 237
eye contact
  avoiding becoming victim of crime, 204
  overview, 115–117
  pointing and, 214
  on Zoom, 99–100
eyebrows, 105
eyes
  facial expressions relying on, 105
  hands over, 213

facial expressions, 93–120
  eye contact, 115–117
  importance of, 101–106
  in infancy and early childhood
    overview, 106–109
    tips for helping, 110–113
  in late childhood
    overview, 114–115
    tips for helping, 118–120

INDEX

facial expressions *(cont.)*
  overview, 48–49
  screen time and, 98–99
  smiling, 93–96
  teaching personal space with, 140–141
  wearing masks, 96–98
  when expert intervention is needed, 120
  Zoom schooling, 99–100
"failure to thrive" syndrome, 28–29
faking feelings, 103
fear, 97
fidgeting, 203, 222–223
Field, Tiffany, 109
"fist point" gesture, 203
flight response, 123
Foote, Tom, 81
four-phase model of relationships, 40–46
  choice phase, 41–42
  deepening phase, 43–44
  initiation phase, 42–43, 83
  personal space boundaries in, 137–138
  smiling during, 95
  transition phase, 44–46, 84
Freud, Sigmund, 29–30
friendships ("chums"), 39–40, 138. *see also* relationships

gait, 202–207
gender
  body language with, 219
  touch style with, 160
Generation Z (Gen Z), 9, 13
gestures
  driving interaction, 51
  learning through screen time, 216
  milestones in early childhood, 213–215
  overview, 202–207
  playing using, 215
Gillentine, Jonathan, 163
giving and showing, 213

glancing, 117
Goldberg, Suzanne B., 11
Goleman, Daniel, 6
grabbing, 213
Graziano, Michael, 123, 128–129
green light/red light game, 135
Greene, Melissa Faye, 29
greetings, 120
  in different cultures, 56
  personal space with, 122
Guilmartin, Kenneth, 80
Gullberg, Marianne, 201

Halberstadt, Amy, 105, 108
Hall, Edward T., 124
hand positions, 197
hands over eyes, 213
happiness, 95–96, 97
Harker, LeeAnne, 95
Harlow, Harry, 150
Head Start program, 76–77, 233
hearing problems, 193
heartbeat rhythm, 76
Helping the Child Who Doesn't Fit In (Nowicki and Duke), 6
Hewes, Gordon, 197
The Hidden Dimension (Hall), 124
Holmqvist, Kenneth, 201
Holt, Daphne, 130
Hope, Joan, 11
Horner, Thomas, 132
hugging, 50, 133
  benefits of, 146
  difficulties during pandemic, 150–151
  impact of teachers, 154
  seeking permission before, 160–161
hypersensitivity to touch, 168

Ice Age, 216
illustrators, 197–198
improv classes, 119–120, 224
incongruent communication, 4
indoor voices, 185–186

INDEX

infancy and infants
  body language in, 210–212
  bond between parents and, 30
  facial expressions in, 106–109
  "failure to thrive" syndrome, 28–29
  fostering healthy nonverbal communication during, 233–234
  how nonverbal language develops in, 34–36, 53
  maternal touch and nurturance with, 150
  personal space in, 132–134
  physical touch in, 157–159
  rhythm in, 76–77
  "still face" experiment, 31–32
  vocalics in, 182–184
infant-directed speech, 183, 184
initiation phase, relationship
  overview, 42–43
  personal space boundaries in, 137–138
  resting face and, 114–115
  rhythm during, 83
  smiling during, 95
interjections, 179
interrupting, 78, 89–90
intimate zone, 124, 141

Japanese culture
  expressions, intensity of, 105
  greetings, 56
joint attention, 108, 214

Keltner, Dacher, 95
kinesics, 54
kiss, blowing, 214
Kraus, Michael, 173
Kringelbach, Morten, 94
Krout, Maurice, 197

late childhood
  body language in
    overview, 217–220
    tips for helping, 221–225

  facial expressions in
    overview, 114–115
    tips for helping, 118–120
  fostering healthy nonverbal communication during, 236–237
  how nonverbal language develops in, 38–40
  personal space in
    overview, 136–139
    tips for navigating in, 139–142
  physical touch in
    overview, 163
    tips for encouraging positive touch in, 165–168
  rhythm in, 82–86
    becoming cognizant of time, 84–86
    tips for helping, 86–90
  vocalics in
    overview, 187–190
    tips for helping, 191–193
Latin American culture, 85
laughter, 187
Laukka, Petri, 181–182
learning communication
  differences between verbal and nonverbal communication, 59–60
  similarities between verbal and nonverbal communication, 53–54
Leipold, Simon, 175–176
Lewis, C. S., 43
life, relationships and, 28–33
Linden, David, 156
listening, 76
loneliness, 9–10
"lower face" emotion, 97

manners, 103
Markman, Ellen, 185
martial arts, 217

INDEX

masks, 49
  facial expressions and, 96–98
  vocalic development and, 180–181
maternal touch, 150
Matsumoto, David, 105
McGlone, Francis, 157
mealtimes, 113
"measure the loaf" gesture, 203
Meeren, Hanneke, 200
Mehrabian, Albert, 33, 176
mental health crisis, 9
Middle Eastern culture
  eye contact in, 117
  space bubbles in, 126
mime classes, 224
mimicking beat, 79
"model and photographer" game, 111
modulation, 190
Moebius syndrome, 101
monotone, 190
Morton, Bruce, 183–184
motherese, 183
mouth, 105
movement therapists, 225
multi-kinesic, 56–57
multilingualism, 56–57, 185
music, 88
Music Together program, 80–82, 88, 217, 225

National Survey of Children's Health, 10
negative feelings, 235
negative self-concept, 35–36
negative touch, 160–161
neurodivergent children and adolescents, 3–4
neurons
  C-touch fibers, 148–149, 157, 166
  peripersonal neurons, 123–124, 129, 133
Neves, Leonor, 174
nodding, 214

nonverbal communication, 25–61
  language of relationships, 25–46
    four-phase model of relationships, 40–46
    how nonverbal language develops, 33–40
    matter of life and death, 28–33
  types of, 47–52
    body language, 51–52
    facial expressions, 48–49
    personal space, 49
    physical touch, 49–50
    rhythm, 48
    vocalics, 50–51
  verbal communication vs.
    differences between, 57–61
    similarities between, 52–57
nursery rhymes, 78, 112
nurturance, 150

object permanence, 213
objectics, 52, 207–210
"one in five" rule, 235–236
oppositional personality disorder, 187–188
outdoor voices, 185–186
Owen, Pamela, 163

pace of speech, 178–179, 190
pain, physical touch and, 145–147
pandemic pandemonium, 13–14
parents
  bond between child and, 30
  choosing friends for young children, 41–42
pausing, in conversation, 57
Pease, Allan, 203
Pei, Mario, 54
peripersonal neurons, 123–124, 129, 133
personal region, 125, 141
personal space, 121–143
  importance of, 122–132
  in infancy and early childhood

INDEX

overview, 132–134
   tips for making visible and concrete in, 134–136
in late childhood
   overview, 136–139
   tips for navigating in, 139–142
observing children at school, 25–26
overview, 49
when expert intervention is needed, 142
Personal Space Day, 142
persuasion, 176
photos, finding facial expressions in, 111
physical abuse, 154
physical touch. *see* touch
pitch, voice, 177–178
playdates, 38
playing
   with infants, 233
   using gestures, 215
pointing, 213–214, 216
positive self-concept, 35
positive touch, 160–161, 163–165
posture
   classification of, 197–198
   in early childhood, 212
   importance of, 202–207
   overview, 51–52
   practicing, 222
power posing, 202–203, 204
practicing facial expressions, 110–111
private body parts, 162–163, 167
public zone, 125, 141
pulling, 213

racial bias, 105–106
reaching, 213
reading, practicing vocalics by, 186
receptive language skills, 55–56
recording voice, 191
regulators, 197–198
relationships, 25–46

facial expressions, importance of, 101–102
four-phase model of, 40–46
   choice phase, 41–42
   deepening phase, 43–44
   initiation phase, 42–43, 83
   transition phase, 44–46, 84
how nonverbal language develops, 33–40
   early childhood phase, 36–38
   infancy, 34–36
   late childhood phase, 38–40
matter of life and death, 28–33
resilience, 29
resonance, 233
resting face, 114–115, 119
resting posture, 219–220
rhythm, 67–91
in early childhood
   Head Start program, 76–77
   tips to help instill in child, 77–79
importance of, 72–76
in infancy, 76–77
Isabel observation study, 67–70
in late childhood, 82–86
   becoming cognizant of time, 84–86
   tips for helping child, 86–90
Music Together program, 80–82
overview, 48
when expert intervention is needed, 90–91
Zoom schooling affecting, 71–72
Rhythm Kids, 81, 88, 225
Rochat, Philippe, 31
Rogers, Fred, 1
Rothman, Alexia, 174
rudeness, 48
Rutter, Michael, 29

sadness, 97
sarcasm, 189, 193
Saturday Night Live skit, 177
scents, 207

INDEX

school, 40–41. *see also* Zoom schooling
  correcting verbal communication at, 59
  friendships transitioning in, 44–45
  in late childhood, 38–39
  physical touch in classroom, 163–165
  showing affection after, 161–162
  as touch-free zones, 155
screen time
  ability to identify emotion and, 15
  adjusting rhythm with, 71–72
  facial expressions and, 98–99
  instilling sense of rhythm and limiting, 79
  learning gestures through, 216
  personal space in cyberspace, 131
second language class, 185
Seinfeld episodes, 177, 205
self-concepts, 35–36
self-disclosure, 43
self-presentation, 224–225
self-soothing, 162
7-38-55 rule, 176
sexual abuse, 154
shaking hands, 56, 166–167
shaking the head, 213
"shhh" gesture, 214
showing and giving, 213
Siegel, Daniel, 233
Silent Messages (Mehrabian), 176
silent orchestra, 63–65
singing, 78–79
six-foot rule, 130
smiling, 93–96, 102
So You Think You Can Dance, 223
social brain, 157
social graces, 103
social interaction
  during early childhood, 38
  making nonverbal mistakes during, 58
social isolation, 10–14. *see also* Zoom schooling

social referencing, 107
social space, 125, 141
space bubbles, 126–128, 134–135
space invaders, 25–26, 129–130
The Spaces between Us (Graziano), 129
sports
  instilling sense of rhythm with, 90
  opportunities for touch in, 166
  teaching body language while watching, 223–224
standing, 222
staring, 116–117
"still face" experiment, 31–32
"stop" gesture, 214, 218, 221
stories, teaching facial expressions through, 113, 118–119
subtle sound patterns, 188
suicidal ideation, 11
Sullivan, Harry Stack, 4, 29–30, 138
superior temporal sulcus, 175–176
synchronicity, 83
synchrony, 190

TED talks, 202–203
temperaments, 73–74
tempos, 88–89
theater performances, 224
theater programs, 119–120, 224
time
  becoming cognizant of, 84–86
  maintaining eye contact and, 116
  teaching children, 87–88
time-management chart, 87
Tomasello, Michael, 212
tone of voice, 33, 178
touch, 145–169
  in classroom, 163–165
  communication through, 147–148
  experience of pain and, 145–147
  importance of, 148–156
  in infancy and early childhood, 108
  overview, 157–159
  tips for introducing to, 159–163

INDEX

in late childhood
    overview, 163
    tips for encouraging positive touch in, 165–168
  overview, 49–50
  when expert intervention is needed, 168
Touch (Linden), 156
transition phase, relationship
  overview, 44–46
  rhythm during, 84
  smiling during, 95
Trehub, Sandra, 183–184
Tronick, Edward, 31
trust, 43
turn-taking
  helping with body language, 215–216
  instilling sense of rhythm
    in early childhood, 77–78
    in late childhood, 89–90
  regulators, 198

Uhls, Yalda, 15
"upper face" emotion, 97

Van Edwards, Vanessa, 203
Van Zant, Alex, 176
verbal communication
  during early childhood, 36–38
  emotional messages transmitted by, 33
  nonverbal communication vs.
    differences between, 57–61
    similarities between, 52–57
virtual interactions, 71–72
vocalics, 171–194
  importance of, 173–182
  in infancy and early childhood
    overview, 182–184
    tips for helping, 184–187
  in late childhood
    overview, 187–190
    tips for helping, 191–193
  overview, 50–51
  types of, 177–180
  when expert intervention is needed, 193–194
volume, voice, 177, 185–186

Waal, Frans de, 56
walking rhythm, 75
walking styles, 204
WALL-E, 216
Watzlawick, Paul, 59
waving, 213, 214
Western culture, 56
whining, 186
white Americans, 105
Wichstrøm, Lars, 15
Willems, Mo, 112
Winfrey, Oprah, 6
World Health Organization, 12

yoga classes, 225
Yow, Quin, 185

zones of personal space, 124–125, 141
Zoom schooling. *see also* school
  affecting rhythm, 71–72
  effort needed to communicate over, 180
  facial expressions over, 99–100
zygomatic nerve, 149

STEPHEN NOWICKI is the Charles Howard Candler Professor of Psychology Emeritus at Emory University. During his fifty years of teaching at Emory University in Atlanta, Dr. Nowicki has served as director of clinical training, head of the Psychological Center, and head of the Counseling Center. He is currently completing a three-year grant in Bristol, England, for the study of the origins of nonverbal abilities and locus of control. A consultant to a variety of businesses, organizations, and public and private educational programs, Nowicki maintains an active clinical practice as a diplomate in psychology.